Anna, Age Eight

The data-driven prevention of childhood trauma and maltreatment

Katherine Ortega Courtney, PhD & Dominic Cappello

Jessica Fox

ISBN-13: 978-1979903073
ISBN-10: 1979903077

Cover by: Bram Meehan

DEDICATION

Throughout this book, we'll tell you the story of eight-year-old Anna, and her deeply troubled mother, Cassandra. Anna is a fictional case informed by our experiences working with several state child welfare departments. The details have been significantly altered to protect her real identity. There are almost 2,000 cases of untimely deaths like Anna's in the United States every year. It is now also estimated that one in eight children will be substantiated as maltreated by age eighteen. Anna represents these children, whose lives ended too soon because of preventable causes. Anna was the catalyst that inspired our writing. Her story was literally the tipping point for us, the event that sealed our commitment to producing this work.

~

For Anna, and all those working tirelessly to prevent the trauma and maltreatment she endured.

CONTENTS

ACKNOWLEDGMENTS

First and foremost, we thank Peter Rice, who crafted our sentences and ensured we would not shy away from controversial concepts, all while giving the book's voice a welcome sharp edge. We also thank Xenia Becher, Yarrott Benz, Paula Brooks, Susan Burgess, Brian Clapier, Sandra Davidson, Laura Davis, Richard Dunks, Jeffrey Escoffier, Bonnie Faddis, Lauri Halderman, Melissa Hardin, Tad Harmon, Joanne Hicks-Campbell, Whitney Johnson, Cathy Kodama, Maya McKnight, Sarah Meadows, Shannon Morrison, Dubra Karnes-Padilla, Mary Ellen O'Neil, Patrice Perrault, Elizabeth Peterson, Dr. Craig Pierce, Heather Race, Faith Russler, Greg Sherrow, Norma Straw, Arianna Trott, Delphine Trujillo, Alan Webber, Ian Wolfley, Katy Yanda and Connecticut's Susan Smith for their invaluable advice, assistance, and friendship. Our work with data leadership was supported by Casey Family Programs, and we offer gratitude to their staff: Susan Smith, Susan Reilly, Malcolm Hightower, Stacie Buchanan, Kirk O'Brien, and Barbara Needell.

Thank you to Dr. Jon Courtney, Dr. Heather Labansat, and Andrew and Evita Ortega for their constant and unwavering support.

And a special thank you to our friends and colleagues in New Mexico, New York City, and Connecticut child welfare, fighting for the children of the world every single day. You are the heroes of this story.

Preface

_____

Waking up from a
bad dream

READING A BOOK about childhood trauma is, in many ways, like waking up from a bad dream. The fog that once obscured this tragic corner of life slowly clears, and the more you learn, the more you see children at risk all over the place, facing adversity and trauma, as you go about your everyday life. Turning the pages of a book on childhood challenges, you may well experience feelings of overwhelming sadness, anger, frustration and hopelessness. You may feel powerless, as though you are single-handedly facing some monstrous thing far too big to confront.

This is a book about how trauma impacts us, our children, our communities, and a nation living through the epidemic. But more importantly, it is also a blueprint for fixing something terribly wrong with our country. What we are proposing is far beyond mere trauma-informed behavioral health care (though that's a vital component). Our proposal is a social moonshot, because that's what's possible and necessary. Our goal is nothing short of radically transforming how we support each community, so that every child grows up, free from trauma, in family-friendly cities and towns.

This book is based on our professional experience working in child welfare, as well as with our community partners from public health, education, behavioral health, youth development and law enforcement. Our insights are informed by everything from educational programs focused on continuous quality improvement, brainstorming sessions with software developers, the tales of street activists, and everything in between. Because we have also endured trauma and witnessed trauma's ravages on families, there are passages in this book that reflect deep frustration with those that block solutions. We do not tiptoe around those in denial, obstructionists, or dinosaur-like power brokers. We strongly question a status quo that has accepted the high rates of childhood trauma and maltreatment with disastrous consequences for all of us. You may find our candor overly caustic, and for that we simply beg your forgiveness in advance.

We seek to challenge the ubiquitous dichotomy of savior vs. victim, to which we all might be easily drawn when looking at traumatized families. This book is not about us versus them – it's about how we are all living together in a traumatized society, and how together we can find a way out. This is also a book about fairness and justice, about doing what's right with the abundant resources we have and hoard. While we promote good government leadership as a critical tool, we also believe in the power of all local communities to be equal partners in a healing process.

We invite you to enter a conversation with us, to explore a variety of interconnected challenges, and to critically analyze how we are raising our children, in this culture, at this time in history. When we say "ending childhood trauma" we mean all children – whether living in city centers, rural hamlets, suburbs, mansions, housing projects or homeless shelters. The biggest question is this: Do we collectively want to solve the epidemic of trauma, or do we keep asking families to solve this problem on their own?

We tell stories over ten chapters that coalesce into a single guide for action. The beginning of our book may be the most challenging, as it asks you to witness and confront the consequences of trauma – something some of our early reviewers described as the equivalent of being doused with a bucket of cold water. Trust that the chapters will weave together to empower the reader – from whatever vantage point one sits.

A prospective editor asked us: "Is this a book for the general public or social workers?" Our response was that it was for both those who work every day with our most traumatized families and a public that knows something is wrong. Both seek an explanation of how adverse childhood experiences impact their lives today. Ending the epidemic of childhood trauma will require that all of us, in all public and private sectors, partner with community leaders across the nation, networking together in very new and strategic ways.

Finally, we write this book after years of working in child welfare, a sector whose tireless staffers serve our nation's most vulnerable and traumatized populations. We have seen the promise of problem-solving through our own Data Leaders and quality improvement program for child welfare, launched in 2015. Far from brain surgery, our Data Leaders Program gives people with good insights the time, space, resources, and support to design and launch their own innovations. After we launched our Resilience Leaders Program to support the prevention of childhood trauma, we continued to see firsthand how problems thought to be unsolvable are taken on by agency and community leadership with creativity and courage.

We can make huge strides toward healing our children, families and communities, and we can do it today. But first, we have to confront some uncomfortable truths about where we stand. We have to question how we currently approach the prevention of childhood trauma. We need to ask who or what is keeping us from using a data-driven, cross-sector, and systemic strategy that is staring us in the face. The trauma of children and their parents is only never-ending because, up until this point, our nation has failed to act.

We love provoking outrage just as much as every other duo of veteran government policy wonks, but given the time and research commitment we've undertaken here, we want to do much more than point out problems. We felt it vital to provide practical steps you can actually take, whether you work in city hall, state government, foundations, child welfare, social services, youth advocacy agencies, schools, socially-engaged software companies, or are a community activist, local blogger, or ordinary citizen. Hence, the unique creation you now hold: A non-fiction documentary of a book that can also serve as a "how to."

We firmly believe that every community can solve problems that were once thought unsolvable. The strategies we propose here are tested by decades of work in and out of government agencies. Some places really are getting it right, and we include here stories and insights from child welfare, public health, and education profess-ionals that illustrate how data can inform effective problem-solving. Often, the stories concern our own work, or people we know.

A gentle warning: If you're not familiar with social work, some of the stories about childhood trauma may be upsetting and emotionally jarring. But we include them, quite simply, because those who don't already work in the field may benefit from a reality check. These are children from neighborhoods just like yours, whether you live in a gated community or that one part of town everybody avoids if they can.

Technical notes: We have changed the names of all children, parents, and staff, in order to respect confidentiality. In some instances, and for the same reasons, we have also changed genders and family make up. Others are composites. Unless you see a full first and last name, those working within the system were quoted with the guarantee that they could remain anonymous, ensuring the most candid observations. We also include personalized vignettes titled "Katherine's Journal" and "Dom's Journal," as a way to relay some personal experiences within our collective story.

Helpful terms

We have worked hard to avoid insider phrases in this book, but a few upfront definitions might be helpful to readers not familiar with some terms used within behavioral health care, child welfare and public health.

Data-driven: Instead of the common government method – decisions based on hunches, what's been done before, or the whim of the director, we base all our work on data. We're swimming in excellent data and research that provides all the information we need to start solving challenges today. And data are far from only quantitative (intimidating numbers). Data are also qualitative and come from the stories and inspiring life experiences of our friends and neighbors.

Cross-sector: Instead of doing our work in isolation or a silo, we reach across the key sectors of the multi-disciplinary public sector to coordinate work. We've identified (later on in the book) ten vital services in ten distinct social sectors that make up a resilient family-friendly community. This means child welfare and public health work in synch with education, youth development, behavioral health care, and job training. We communicate across our agencies to assess challenges, plan with research, implement action and measure progress.

Systemic: Instead of looking at only one particular part of the challenge facing families, we approach our work by looking at the health of an entire community system. The magnitude of the problem requires that we take into thoughtful consideration all the interrelationships and interdependencies among the parts of the whole, whether it be our own organization or the communities we focus on. Technology makes systemic work, internally and externally, transparent. For meaningful change, systemic thinking is required.

Data Leaders programs: These are continuous quality improvement programs housed within government and non-governmental agencies to train the workforce in using data to solve problems. These programs build collaboration between data specialists, upper management, training staff, and the field workers, in order to improve outcomes for the populations their agencies serve.

Trauma-informed care: This is a strength-based framework in the social sectors and behavioral health care that is responsive to the impact of emotional trauma in children and adults. This approach emphasizes physical and emotional safety for both service providers and survivors and creates opportunities for survivors to rebuild a sense of control over their lives and a feeling of empowerment. It is important to note that trauma-informed care is not the same thing as a data-driven and cross-sector strategy for preventing and treating adverse childhood experiences and trauma.

Chapter One

_____

Comfortably numb

Anna's Story

Anna was like many of us at age eight, growing up with adversity. Her particular adverse childhood experiences came from living in households where adults misused substances and lived with untreated mental illness. Then more adversity arrived. We will detail Anna's story, a life that ended far too early, throughout the course of this book, but for now, we ask you to think back for just a moment to reflect on your childhood and how parts of it may have mirrored her story. You may not relate at all to any of her circumstances, but that actually puts you in a minority.

FAR AWAY FROM YOU, on the other side of town, or the other side of the tracks, children live out perfectly miserable lives. If you're a social worker, of course, this is what you face every day. If, on the other hand, you are like the rest of the American public, you take notice once in a while, perhaps engaging in a bit of head shaking. But for the most part, these boys and girls are out of sight and out of mind. This book is not just about those kids.

This book is about all our kids, including your children, your sister's children, and your neighbor's children. It is about everyone who was once a child. It's about what goes on in your or your neighbor's home that nobody knows about. It is about headlines and cries for help that, try as we might, we cannot escape:

Eva, age two, was left in a motel room as her mom passed out from the drugs.

A group is lobbying to reinstate the death penalty just to 'fry' the mother who killed her four-year-old son, Derek.

Why didn't the school and neighbors know that six-year-old Dana was at risk for being abused by her parents?

A mother left her two-year-old daughter, Angela, with a boyfriend, who would later drown her, complaining that the little girl just cried too much.

How could a 12-year-old, Doug, literally starve to death over the course of months, in front of his teacher?

People are outraged that the prison system let someone out on probation without knowing he was a sociopath – letting him brutally murder his new girlfriend's ten-year-old daughter.

Here is the tip of the iceberg, but if we are lucky enough to escape the most violent possibilities, we still bolster the foundation. We are all packed together into this small island planet, floating about the universe, trying to make something of our fate and all these problems. This book is about all of us.

Which brings us to a reasonable question: What kind of sick society are we? How is it that the world's oldest constitutional democracy manages to send railroads across a continent and rocket ships to the moon, all in the process of becoming the richest nation in the history of time, but also plays host to the routine rape, starvation, burning, and beating of children? Why are so many kids scarred, born addicted, and generally traumatized? Not every tragedy can be prevented, of course, but this? This is our best effort? Surely, we may wonder, all these bruised, beaten, abused and murdered children need not show up on the nightly news, week after week, in such horrifying quantities.

Feel like looking away at this point? You're not alone. We're happy to muster our full attention for any number of causes and passing memes, from the entirely vapid to the occasionally consequential. But when it comes to the magnitude of childhood trauma and maltreatment, we prefer to live in blissful denial.

That's a stain on our collective moral character, to be sure, but the "strategy" also backfires spectacularly. We all know traumatized kids and their problems don't go away just because we stop thinking about them. They share playgrounds and classrooms and church youth groups with our kids, and when they grow up to be adults, they share our workplaces, sell us groceries, serve as our elected representatives, and marry into our families. They are everywhere. They are legion. They might be even be you.

In the best-case scenario, the trauma of abuse and neglect that these kids suffered is in the past. But we need not read William Faulkner novels to know that the past is never dead, and in fact is not even past. Humans don't work like that. Emotionally healthy people who are treated well through life tend to treat others well, in an emotionally healthy way, but the opposite is also true. Whatever happened to those kids that we try not to think about – whenever it happened – it will brush off with every human interaction, and then some little piece of it will have happened to you, and to all of us.

We pay for this blissful denial with lots of cold, hard cash. Besides the government agencies designed to help kids in the thick of it, there are the extra cops and prisons to backstop the failures, and the welfare state that, even if it can't solve the underlying problem, pays to ensure that people don't starve (mostly) and have a place to live (more or less). Traumatized kids also have quite understandable problems learning, so the schools spend more of your money on extra help, sometimes stealing time from your kids in the process. As adult survivors, those with untreated trauma will be less economically productive, hanging invisible weights on the GDP at large, and probably on your workplace in particular.

When this trauma inflicted on children rises to the level of a fatality, especially one almost tailor-made for TV, we are all collectively mortified. We express horror and outrage, and there is much moaning and gnashing of teeth. But like an unstable isotope, that energy seems to have a half-life of only a day or two. By next week, it's just a light hum in the background. Until the next fatality, when the process begins again, because according to the newscasters and the officials they interview, there is no clear way to stop it.

We want to stop it, of course, but where do we even begin? Where do we start to tackle this multi-generational, multi-faceted issue of childhood safety, and its aftereffects that roll on through time? Which agency head can we haul before a legislative panel for an angry reckoning and very public shaming? Who can we fire? And is it safe to divide blame among crazy parents, unobservant teachers, and lazy social workers?

Not quite.

"When children are harmed, society cries out for justice," says Melissa Hardin, who managed a county office for New Mexico Child Protective Services. "But for whom? It's too late for the young child. So society looks to assign blame for an oversight made by someone, somewhere. Surely, an adult in contact with this child should have seen something and acted."

Thus responsibility is removed from the many and placed on the shoulders of a few overburdened people who can't change the past and who, until the story broke, were the only ones who cared anyway. Whatever guilt we felt from the blissful ignorance is thusly assuaged.

That is obviously a terrible way to approach this. We all own a piece of the mess, and blaming a few people we set up to fail won't get us anywhere. This is an epidemic, and we should generally avoid bringing out the worst in people if we're going to solve anything. During the AIDS crisis, for example, there was plenty of ugly talk about quarantines and "identifying" those infected, perhaps barring them from certain jobs. The compassionate, sensible solutions ultimately won out, but it was "touch-and-go" there for a while.

We're all responsible

So in the interest of keeping this on track, let's be clear that all of us collectively allow unsafe childhoods, filled with adversity, to remain a standard feature of these United States. We do not control the actions of one broken person doing harm to one child, but we do influence the surrounding environment that is the single biggest predictor of whether the harm will come. Change will arrive only when we who are ultimately responsible for the situation demand it.

What on earth would that change look like? We barely have a picture of that, despite living in a society obsessed with numerical metrics that fancies itself as forward thinking. With kids, we tend to measure what's going right, like satisfactory math scores, school attendance, graduation rates, and college admissions percentages. These numbers are great to have, but they don't tell the full story. What's missing is the information about the people who ended up on the other side of the hoped-for outcome. Were they safe from violence and assault? Did they live in homes that prominently featured substance abuse, untreated mental illness, or neglect and malnutrition? We need to measure success, to be sure, but to do so correctly we must also measure failure.

Chapter Two

_____

An epidemic we prefer

not to see

Anna's Story

To be eight years old is usually a fun, happy, safe harbor of a pastime. Toilet training and other indignities of the toddler life are vanquished, and the parental surveillance state is showing some welcome initial signs of relaxation. At school, there are a couple of grades to look down on. You've cracked the adult's secret code of spelling out words to evade understanding, and signs around town suddenly make much more sense. Adolescence is coming, of course, but you're still pretty busy being a kid. All in all, it's a great age.

It was not so for Anna. In her eight years, she had racked up just as many episodes in the custody of her state's child welfare system. Returned again to her very troubled mother, Cassandra, she celebrated a birthday with a few small toys and, we can only hope, some quantity of good cheer. If she did so, it would have been about the last high point she would ever know. A few days later, Cassandra and her boyfriend beat Anna to death in a drug-fueled, mental illness-influenced rage.

The murder might actually have kept a low profile had it not happened in a particularly slow news week. With little else to report on, the news media saw to it that the affair dominated all manner of nightly newscast, morning broadsheet, and social media feed. After the initial shock, the story shifted to questions like this: Why on earth did Child Protective Services, an agency allegedly designed to stop such tragedies, return this poor girl to a mother with a well-documented and deeply troubling history? The outcry was loud and lengthy, and caught the attention of state legislators. For a time, Anna became the face of child abuse, and because the incident occurred right before a big election year, many new and reactive bills soon issued forth from the state house to make sure Something Like This Would Never Happen Again.

ANNA IS ON THE EXTREME END OF THE SPECTRUM that tracks children's lives from safe to unsafe. Hers is the type of dramatic, and thus newsworthy, case that people are most likely to hear about through the media. But while the fracas was not lacking for empathy and hearts in the right place, there was no context. Was Anna an anomaly? If so, how much of one? Would childhood fatality numbers, even if they could be acquired, tell a comprehensive story?

Short answer: One data point is not-at-all comprehensive.

Longer answer: As a media-consuming citizenry, we see made-for-TV child fatalities as islands in a vast ocean. They pop up from time to time, and we as a society notice them, learn the details, get angry, and try to compare them to other islands we've seen before. But this proves to be a fruitless exercise, because what we're not seeing is more important. Only underneath the water's surface will you find the once invisible answers.

Dive in, and you'll see an elaborate mountain range built of physical, emotional, and sexual abuse – small, everyday incidents that rarely inspire attention from government agencies or the news media. Look closer, and you'll see submerged peaks made of maltreatment at the hands of adults with untreated mental illness, the prevalence of domestic violence in a home, and rampant substance misuse. Every rock on that mountain range is something going horribly wrong for a child, and we have a formal term for such things: adverse childhood experiences, or ACEs. This is the foundation of Anna's homicide.

Usually, things go wrong for kids in a way that we can't see. Sometimes, that's because an opaque government agency turns a blind eye. Sometimes, it's our own fatigue and apathy. Sometimes, there is simply nobody to see horrible things that happen in isolation. But whatever the excuse, a soft conspiracy soon emerges to keep the trauma underwater and out of sight. When the abuse happens in wealthier families (the "one percent" are not immune to all forms of childhood trauma and maltreatment), they can use lawyers and political connections as blinders, often successfully hiding from the authorities. But even for the middle class, working class, and poor families, a culture of secrecy and shame is nearly as effective. So trauma keeps happening to kids, every moment of every day. Only once in a great while, enough things go enough wrong in a dramatic-enough way on a slow-enough news week, and it builds the mountain high enough to break through the surface, forming an island in the public consciousness. But not very often.

About trauma

From a strictly medical point of view, trauma means only a serious injury to a person's body. But for our purposes, it can be more broadly defined as very difficult or unpleasant experiences that cause someone to have mental or emotional problems. Lots of these problems end with the passage of a little time and a couple of heart-to-hearts with good friends. Routine romantic breakups in high school work like that, as does a troubling failure to make the football team. But all too often, more dramatic trauma causes problems that continue to hamper normal life, long after the trauma itself has ended. These experiences become stubborn emotional wounds, and they hamper a child's ability to trust, attach emotionally to others, and do all the other basic entry-level tasks of a healthy and successful life. Like any other wound, leaving the business of healing to the passage of time only works in the least serious circumstances, clichés to the contrary notwithstanding.

Trauma is so pervasive in our society that it takes a rather comprehensive survey just to delineate the types of traumatic events children are experiencing. It's called the Adverse Childhood Experiences Study, and it may have already been deployed in a community near you. It is essentially a checklist of potentially traumatic events, both large and less large. Some of the surveyed experiences are brushed off by cynics as normal, perhaps even character building. But for most of these experiences, basically everyone already agrees that they are terrible, horrible, no-good and very bad.

The Adverse Childhood Experiences Study (ACE Study) was first conducted by Kaiser Permanente and the Center for Disease Control and Prevention (CDC) in 1995. It used a longitudinal methodology to assess health outcomes of participants. Hundreds of presentations and scientific articles have looked at the pervasive effects of ACEs. (The original study was published in the American Journal of Preventive Medicine in 1998 by Felitti et. al, titled "Relationship of Childhood Abuse and Household Dysfunction to Many of the Leading Causes of Death in Adults: The Adverse Childhood Experiences (ACE) Study.") Despite the tongue twister of a title, it was groundbreaking research that changed the way adult health and childhood experiences were understood. The ACE Study also illuminated how cycles of trauma and health are passed from generation to generation. It called for society-wide change to improve the quality of household and family environments during childhood. Family based-primary prevention, such as home visiting, was needed on a large and long-term scale, the study said.

That was two decades ago, and there are still no comprehensive strategies, at a federal or state level, to reduce ACEs. We have an overflowing child welfare system that deals with the extreme impact of ACEs, but we have yet to invest in these upstream approaches in any significant way.

DOM'S JOURNAL

I was invited to a Seattle software company to present an overview of our ACEs prevention strategies to the staff, who also worked at a foundation dedicated to various good works. I discussed the original study done two decades earlier, the ACEs surveys revealing the high rates of many forms of household dysfunction and maltreatment, and the consequences to all family members. When I was done, a twenty-something program manager asked with earnestness, "If this problem is as serious as you say for as long as you say, why don't we ever hear about it?" His question is one I grapple with every day. What kind of society lives in a state of near-complete denial of such well-documented suffering? More importantly, why have we failed to heed the recommendations of the ACE Study authors?

What we're talking about

So, what exactly are ACEs? The list includes, in no particular order: physical abuse, emotional abuse, physical neglect, emotional neglect, sexual abuse, witnessing domestic violence, living in a household with someone who is mentally ill, living in a household with someone who abuses alcohol and/or drugs (legal or not), having a family member sent to prison, and having parents who separated or divorced.

Being social creatures, humans are basically the sum total of whatever they've been taught to be. Sure, genetics are a factor – sometimes a very big one, but basically, we're the sum of our inputs. If we have healthy, positive inputs from parents, peers, teachers, faith groups, sports leagues, or whatever, we generally turn out pretty well. But if our inputs are a series of hopelessly negative experiences, like that list of traumas, we're in trouble. Serious trouble.

This should not come as a surprise, but the levels of adverse childhood experiences like those listed above can predict to a degree all kinds of risky behavior later on in life. Put too many of them into a childhood, and pretty soon the risk of suicide, alcoholism, illicit drug use, prescription drug misuse, smoking, severe obesity, depression, physical inactivity, risky sexual behaviors, and sexually transmitted diseases go through the roof. Garbage in, garbage out. Trauma in, trauma out.

The cost of all that is not to be underestimated, because while others do most of the suffering, the rest of us get to pay for it, and not just with money. People going through the trauma of adverse childhood experiences are more likely to fill our jails, lower the productivity of our workforce, inhibit learning in schools, overtax our emergency rooms, get addicted to drugs, commit crimes, and end up lost on the streets. The cost, in money alone, is huge and is borne by every taxpayer, everywhere. And that's not counting the lowered quality of life from merely existing in a society with those realities.

With such high emotional and financial costs, how can it be that most of the American public, and the elected officials that report to them, are not especially informed or motivated to act on the horrible childhoods that are causing so many of our problems? One reason surely is that many of us lead healthy, productive, crime-free lives despite some past emotional trauma, and we're not quite willing to explain away the poor decisions of others by pinning it all on the obstacles we successfully navigated. If a kid gets beat mercilessly and later, as an adult, starts breaking into houses to support a drug habit, the cause and effect relationship is far from direct. It's much easier and more intuitive to believe that such a relationship doesn't exist, and that we're just dealing with bad people and their character flaws. This phenomenon is so ingrained in humans that psychologists have a name for it: Fundamental Attribution Error. Complaining about other people's bad behavior is satisfying, because it absolves us of responsibility and highlights our own honorable goodness all in one neatly-wrapped egotistical package.

But the reason that line of thinking doesn't scan is the simple fact that different people respond to different things in very different ways. One family counselor, Alice, saw this once through two clients who both had high-functioning alcoholic mothers: "I recall being nervous around her when she was intoxicated," one client reported. "It was not pleasant but I wouldn't call it traumatic." The other client was not so lucky: "She found herself unable to be around people – including family and friends – drinking alcohol," Alice told us. "She tenses up and begins to feel scared and traumatized."

One experience, two very different results, and that's humanity for ya. Some people can eat whatever they want and stay thin. George Burns smoked like a chimney and lived to 100. Yet this is not proof that you should take up cigars and supersized meals at McDonalds, just as it is not an argument that people can suck it up and get over whatever is ailing their minds. With adverse childhood experiences, every little bit hurts, and over time, things add up.

Besides, many adverse childhood experiences are far, far worse than getting yelled at few times too many. We've all heard about messy divorces, for example, that leave a mark on kids long after they're adjudicated (though often marks of differing severity). And while the behavior of heavy drinkers is usually harmless and socially acceptable enough, sometimes it turns to yelling, hitting, and breaking things.

And that's just the allegedly minor end of the spectrum. Children on the other side often rack up five, six, or dozens of adverse experiences, and their trauma may well accumulate into lifelong mistrust of others, failure to thrive at school, unhealthy parenting, addiction, and a thousand other things that are not your problem unless you interact with people through your family members, neighbors, co-workers, or romantic partners. Their untreated trauma can become yours. The aftershocks of this trauma spread like a virus, resetting human social relations for the worse as they go. We all face adversity in childhood, and we tend to think whatever we faced was normal, but many of these experiences we dismiss at our peril. The emotional costs are high, especially when put on a high-interest, long-term payment plan known as "not dealing with it."

What a pity, in fact, that adverse childhood experiences are not actually viruses. If they were, the Centers for Disease Control would long ago have recognized them as an epidemic and marshalled a full-scale national response to stop the spread at all costs. We would fight the scourge with all the patriotic fervor and open wallets that we funneled into the moon shot and World War II. Instead, adverse childhood experiences are kept secret and stigmatized, hiding in plain sight.

A cycle we must end at all costs

Anna's story had some unusual staying power. The slow news week certainly helped, but soon all sorts of lurid details were spilling out and propelling the story forward. Cassandra, the mother, was quickly pilloried as a monster, as was her boyfriend. We heard stories about relatives who knew something was not right yet didn't speak out, a child welfare system so overburdened it was described as being constructed with "duct tape and chewing gum," and everything else that would hold our attention long enough to bridge another lucrative commercial break. It just kept coming and coming.

What we did not hear, and what we are still waiting for, was an examination of the story's root causes. No investigative journalist dug into how Cassandra, and people like her, could possibly go so wrong. Had they bothered, they would have found a laundry list of adverse childhood experiences that set her up to fail – a series of bad inputs leading to bad outputs.

We know that normal, healthy people do not get up in the morning and beat their kids to death, so what was going on with Anna's mother? And what can we do today to prevent stuff like this happening tomorrow? Do we need to have a long series of meetings at the state capitol to reexamine some ungodly number of procedures and statutes that deal with this sort of thing? Are various agency directors going to need to get with the program or get out? Do impeachment proceedings for elected leaders need to begin?

The answer is, of course, yes, and we'll have more on that later. For now, suffice it to say that such a narrative would be thoroughly unsatisfying and would not make for great TV. So what if Cassandra and every other high profile parent homicide case in the last ten years was abused as a child? So what if Cassandra had parents who felt unable to do anything as she took up drinking and hard drugs at 12, or whatever the terrible dossier of her life would reveal. *She killed her daughter. And therefore, she is a monster and that is the end of the story.* Pointing out past trauma is irrelevant at best, and a sick/twisted effort to defend child murder at worst.

So that, fellow Americans, is the cycle in a nutshell. Kids get damaged, become adults, damage their kids, and provoke blind rage from the rest of us. We're angry, but we basically stand by and do nothing about a broken system, while more kids get hurt, become adults, have kids, provoke outrage, and so on and so forth. Rinse and repeat. Take your pick from a menu of ten essential traumatic elements that we already know about, and know how to prevent, and slowly that vast underwater mountain range is built anew.

And again, there's a lot of stuff on that list that, especially if it's an isolated incident, kids can recover from without ever getting on the evening news. There are plenty of hard-working, tax-paying, highly successful people out there with healthy families who muddled through horrendous adverse childhood experiences. Once in a while, someone with a hideous portfolio of ACEs wins a Nobel Prize or records a platinum record, and you'll definitely hear about it, but not because it's common. Common stuff doesn't make the news.

This is a game of odds stacked against the traumatized, and they're losing, along with the rest of us who share a country with them. One adverse childhood experience can be enough to send your life into a tailspin that ends up, one way or another, affecting everyone else in society. Pile on a few more, and society's infection keeps growing. This wastes human potential, squanders money, and diminishes the quality of life for everybody.

But it's a big, depressing problem, so on most days we do our best to ignore it and tolerate its consequences. Somebody we know becomes the victim of a minor petty crime, and we duly commiserate, but we probably do not break that crime down to its component parts, which most likely included addictions brought to you in part by adverse childhood experiences. If people at work are causing all kinds of drama to the point of lowering productivity, we will rage against them and their stupidity, ignoring the pile of adverse childhood experiences they carry when they punch in every morning. We spend day after day ranting about them and the problems they cause, because like Anna's mom, they too are monsters, albeit of lower rank.

Unhelpful though this narrative may be, fine. For the sake of argument, let's run with it: The drunk driver in a stolen car who tboned you – monster. The homeless guy and criminal justice system regular who looks terrible and is causing a ruckus while making a mess of the sidewalk – monster. Anna's mom – monster. Monsters all. It's the monster mash of life we call modern society.

But a quick question: Since we usually know the component parts of this criminal, anti-social, or merely obnoxious behavior, and we have some pretty good ideas for removing it from the equation, who here is the bigger monster: The monsters themselves, or the larger society that sets the table of benign neglect, knowing full well what will happen. It seems that the only non-monsters are perhaps the very social workers who get blamed when things go wrong. At least they are trying.

This talk of monsters is just words. Our actions, on the other hand, indicate that we see the effects of this crisis – from the annoyances we deal with every day, to the trainloads of tax dollars we spend, to the dead body of an eight-year-old child – as the tolerable-enough cost of doing business in the Richest. Country. Ever.

We can't afford to do this anymore. The trauma next door is an affront to human potential, an anchor around the neck of economic growth, and a guarantee that everyone, history of childhood adversity and trauma or not, will keep suffering.

Chapter Three

_____

Software, eggshells, and minefields: Illustrating the problem in all its shame

Anna's Story

After Anna's death, an internal review spotted a boring but critical problem with the way Child Protective Services handled the case: Her files (all eight of them) were not easily accessible to staff. These case files represented cold hard information – qualitative and quantitative data from interviews and narratives that thoroughly described Anna's lack of safety. But that information was hidden from the people in charge of preventing exactly what happened. It's entirely possible that bad management of paperwork, and the resulting failure to compile critical information in the right place, cost Anna her life. Before they are solved, problems must first be illuminated.

WHAT DO WE KNOW? We know the childhood trauma and maltreatment problem exists, we know that it is horrible, and we know that it touches every community regardless of race, creed, class, or color. We know that some communities are worse off than others. We also, believe it or not, know how to prevent it, or at least take a big bite out of it. We have the know-how and capacity to treat survivors through established protocols that come standard in trauma-savvy mental health care. We have psychologists, social workers, psychiatrists, family support programs, hospitals, schools, and child welfare agencies. They work in modern buildings with first-world plumbing and electricity. That's the hardware – the obvious, tangible, visible stuff – and all things considered, we're in okay shape in this department. It's not quite big enough, staffwise, in many localities, but it's a promising start to build on.

What we do not have, we argue, is the right software. The people who work in those buildings do not have the right collection of those boring-yet-important tools to do their jobs right: proper protocols, processes, training, and technology. We also lack a comprehensive and intuitive picture of all the component parts of the problem – something that we can use to assess, plan, act, and evaluate our way to a solution. We need something so simple that not even a politician can fail to understand it.

You could be forgiven for thinking this state of affairs is odd, because nearly two decades into this century, the United States is pretty much crushing it in the software department. We're especially good at taking vast, disbursed pieces of isolated and inaccessible information and whooshing them into beautiful and intuitive user experiences. We have many names for those systems, including Facebook, Twitter, Airbnb, and Uber. They've all changed our lives, but they were not hardware revolutions. Twitter is basically just a clever amalgamation of email and the bulletin board at the grocery store. Airbnb is just a series of classified ads with instant payment and delivery. Amazon is the Sears catalog from 1963, plus speed and variety.

These companies didn't invent any hardware, but they did reorganize the software and change the world. We believe the same principle applies to the world of government agencies tasked with protecting, nurturing and educating our children (including child welfare, public health, education, law enforcement, and our judicial systems). Because they, for the most part, are stuck in invisible silos far from public scrutiny, many people who work in the agencies, whose functions are vital to preventing trauma, have not been given the resources, training, or freedom to experiment that drives the sort of software progress we've seen in ride hailing and social media. Ditto for our mental health system, and the social bulwarks that seek to prevent trauma from ever happening, like preschools, parent education, and youth mentoring programs.

When software saves lives

We have a software problem, but how do software problems get fixed? Let's take a look at what Airbnb did.

People have been renting rooms for a very long time, but it was never a very efficient process. Back in the day, you had to personally walk around town and collect data points about room availability, or perhaps pick up such information from friends or acquaintances. Besides taking forever, the inefficiency also yielded some disappointing results, as Mary and Joseph found out a little over

2,000 years ago. And short of personally touring a room, there wasn't much hope of getting a sense of the quality of a place.

Over time, vacancy signs, the standardization of chains, guidebooks, phonebooks (to say nothing of phones) made this process easier, but not by much. You could still easily arrive in a town and find there was no room at the inn. Or you might find that the room was a dump, something you might have known if you lived in the town or had friends there, but of course that probably would have negated the original need for a room. And many people who would be happy to rent out a room were out of the larger loop, stuck with the local market and classified ads.

Along came the internet, and hotel booking sites, which often allowed us to see pictures of the rooms, and get a sense of the place without calling up and grilling some hapless clerk about the breakfast buffet. That was an improvement, of course, but pictures can lie, and average citizens with a spare room were still out of luck.

Fundamentally, the problem was about efficiency and visibility. There was a demand for non-hotel places to sleep, and there was plenty of hardware available in the form of guesthouses and extra rooms to spare, but potential customers couldn't see the whole picture. The data points – who was renting, how much – were fundamentally obscured from the people who could use the information, so the right hand did not really know what the left hand was doing. Finding a place to sleep in a different town or (God help you) a foreign country remained a serious pain.

When you get right down to it, Airbnb just did a massive organizing job. They went around and sucked up data about vacancies, prices, Wi-Fi availability, user reviews, and whether a place was dog friendly, and presented it on a web site in an attractive and intuitive way. Airbnb members and hosts created charming profiles with photos and videos to help you get to know them. They established a few new procedures for efficiently checking in and out of the places, and how to pay for it all. And most importantly, they built in a comprehensive system of continuous quality improvement: Those renting rooms get rated by guests, and vice versa. Under those circumstances, problems are likely to be dealt with quickly and efficiently, as though they are solving themselves.

What finding a room has to do with protecting kids

Our argument is that systems we have to help traumatized kids, and the systems that keep them from getting harmed in the first place, can work the same way. There may be a lot of actors out there, but if we can get the right data together and tell the story of keeping all children safe as simply and intuitively as possible, solutions will become pretty obvious soon enough. Add a few good procedures and a permanent quality control mechanism, and you're on your way to excellence and safer kids.

So, everybody huddle in for a cheer, because we're gonna collect us some data! Sounds fun, right? Maybe even heroic? Who can't get fired up by platoons of people in poorly-lit offices squinting at spreadsheets, giving every impression that they would do well to spend the afternoon at the beach?

We get it. It's not sexy at all. But like phytoplankton, carbon atoms, and the alphabet, it's nothing less than the foundation for the entire solution. Good data is super-duper amazingly important, because it lets us dive into that ocean mentioned above and see every contour of the mammoth underwater mountain range of a problem we're dealing with. It guides our actions and helps us avoid potential catastrophes.

Over the course of this book, we'll talk a lot about data and how it can illustrate (and thus provide the basis for action on) the many component parts of the childhood trauma problem. But for now, let's take a look at the national picture: A data set called the 320 million people in the United States of America.

Using numbers from the U.S. Department of Health and Human Services, we've added up the 2015 numbers (the latest year the public can access easily) for all the reports of suspected child maltreatment called into call centers. It tells us this: 4.0 million calls. Of those reports, 2.2 million were screened into some kind of formal system and sent for investigation by one of our 50 state child welfare systems. (Note: A report can include allegations for more than one child.) The investigations involved 3.4 million children, which is up significantly from 2010. Of those maltreatment cases, authorities classified 75 percent as neglect, 17 percent as physical abuse, and 8 percent as sexual abuse.

Add it all up over the years, as some researchers did in a Journal of American Medical Association article from August 2014, ("The Prevalence of Confirmed Maltreatment Among US Children, 2004-2011"), and it turns out that one in eight children will become formally involved with the child welfare system by age 18. If you're African-American, the number jumps to one in five. For Native Americans, it is one in seven. And that's just neglect and abuse that attracts the attention of the authorities. We are not even beginning to measure the childhood trauma that will never be seen by an investigator.

But while the majority of traumatized children never go near the child welfare system, that doesn't mean they aren't at great risk. We need to dig deeper to truly understand what the hell is happening within our families. So we must unearth new troves of data, from public health departments, law enforcement, domestic violence shelters, and the Centers for Disease Control and Prevention. We can also get data on divorces, child poverty, and incarceration from the Census Bureau and other state sources. Gradually, a much clearer picture of the lives of infants, children, youth, and their parents begins to emerge, and the underwater mountain range gets a bit less blurry. Turns out a majority of our kids are stuck somewhere on that continuum, in varying degrees of peril. But more on that later.

For sheer comprehensiveness in "Data Set America," it doesn't get any better than the Adverse Childhood Experiences Study we mentioned earlier. This provides an estimate, like an opinion poll in a political campaign, so while it's not as exact as the physical count on election day, it gives us a pretty good idea of what's going on out there. As data nerds, we're huge fans of the ACE Survey, and we wish we could administer it to every student in every grade in every school in the country every year, as well as to parents and anybody thinking about becoming one. We enjoy daydreaming about what a treasure trove of useful, life-saving data that would provide, but alas, the politics make it impractical. Still, various people and organizations have already administered the survey at reasonably large scales – like with groups of patients in clinical settings. A few states have surveyed a representative sample of the general population over the phone.

We think the survey is such a useful tool that we're going to spend most of the rest of the chapter dissecting all ten questions in detail. Then we'll share the results from a few statewide surveys. We think you'll agree that these questions are indeed the foundation for understanding the problem, and the first logical step in solving it.

The ACE Study Questions
Ten questions, a clear picture, and a fresh start

NOTE: We're not focusing much on the technical aspects of scoring the survey, but suffice it to say that it counts ACEs up and assigns a "score," which is a good basis for a rough determination of risk for populations. It allows us to say things like "based on the data, people with six or more ACEs are more likely to experience challenges such as...." But below, we're just exploring the topics the survey questions bring up.

ONE: *Did a parent or other adult in the household often or very often push, grab, slap, or throw something at you? Or ever hit you so hard that you had marks or were injured?*

As you might imagine, the answers to this question fall on very different parts of a wide spectrum. Those who answer "yes" may have been pushed once or twice, or they may have suffered routine physical abuse for many years.

"I had a client who was sharing custody of her two children, ages three and six, with her ex-husband," reported Andy, a counselor at a community health center. The ex-husband had remarried, started a new drug habit, and when the kids spent a few nights at his house, they never slept well. "When my client pressed her son for more information, he said it was because his younger sister would cry at bedtime and their father would go in the room and hit her on the bottom for not falling asleep right away," Andy said.

It took some negotiation and several months, but eventually the two parents reached an agreement on how the kids would be punished without hitting, and the problem was solved, likely without permanent damage.

The same could not be said for Joanna, a nine-month-old taken by her mother to the emergency room with a fractured skull and no explanation. "The other child, three-year-old Stevie, stated that 'hitting' occurred in the home with mom and her boyfriend," Dianna, a social worker with Child Protective Services, told us. "Mother continued to deny anything was wrong. Both children were placed in custody due to the unexplained injury."

Those kids were placed in the custody of their grandparents, though later, after a treatment program, the mother had a chance to petition to get them back. A bad situation, to be sure, but at least the kids had the advantage of stable grandparents who would intervene in a pinch.

But that doesn't always work either.

"One of the toughest cases I've worked on was a case with a grandma who had been raising her grandchildren ... in a home with their extremely abusive uncle," said Alice, a Child Protective Services social worker. "I worked with them for six-plus months and never saw any change in thinking by grandma. She did not believe the children were really fearful of their uncle and said toughening them up made them better kids."

We could fill this entire book with responses to and analysis of this question alone. There's a pretty wide spectrum of physical abuse, and people react to it in very different ways. All in all, it turns the jobs of CPS investigators into a series of very delicate and very challenging judgement calls.

TWO: Did a parent or other adult in the household often or very often swear at you, insult you, put you down, or humiliate you? Or act in a way that made you afraid that you might be physically hurt?

Listen to the stories at domestic violence shelters, and you'll quickly find that it's often the threat of physical violence, rather than the violence itself, that causes the trauma. When kids are on the receiving end of these threats or humiliations, or when they see one parent inflicting them on a sibling or the other parent, it can cause problems that may never wind up as part of a conversation at a domestic violence shelter, but leave a mark nonetheless.

Mara, a counselor at a community health center, says this is very common: "Many clients talk about their experiences growing up in a home where they were told to go away because they were in the way, or called 'stupid,' 'idiot,' or 'useless' by their caretakers," she told us. "Some clients indicate their parents were under a lot of stress and didn't know how to deal with them as children, while others say their parents never wanted them. These experiences of emotional abuse impact people deeply and can impact their lifelong beliefs about people and the world."

Mary, a counselor, shared what she saw as a very common and unsettling problem in families: "My client, Davis, talked about his dad who worked on the road most of the time, but when we came home, he was tired and very angry. We were walking on eggshells when he was around, waiting for him to blow up at our mom or us."

THREE: *Did an adult or person at least five years older than you ever touch or fondle you or have you touch their body in a sexual way? Or attempt, or actually have, oral, anal, or vaginal intercourse with you?*

This question aims to explore whether a young person felt abused or traumatized by sexual activity with an older person, while trying to avoid the various "what ifs" presented by wildly different age-of-consent laws around the country. All children need to be protected from predatory adults who would use their power to intimidate and control, and if the five-year age difference is a bit arbitrary, we feel it's nonetheless a useful and simple line of demarcation after which problems with power dynamics get exponentially worse.

Sexual abuse occurs in many forms, and can result in either short-term or life-long consequences, and everything in between. That was the case with Esperanza, who at age 14 had fallen asleep in front of the TV she had been watching with her 19-year-old brother and his best friend, Juan, long a fixture around the house. "She remembered waking up to Juan touching her chest," said Trina, a counselor at a community health center. "She said she didn't know if he was awake or not and didn't know how to react, so she let him put his hand down her pajamas. Esperanza's brother woke up and shook Juan, telling him he should go to bed. Juan suddenly stopped. After this event Esperanza experienced intense symptoms of anxiety and reported having difficulty being alone with men."

It's not hard to imagine Esperanza working through that trauma on her way to a healthy, normal life. But sadly, there is another side to this spectrum.

"The hardest case I've ever had was when a 13-year-old girl named Sandra was raped by her stepfather while her mother (high on heroin) watched and encouraged it as a punishment," said Betty, a Child Protective Services social worker. "Sandra became pregnant with her stepfather's child. After the criminal investigation, the stepfather and mother were sent to jail. Sandra was living with her grandmother, who was trying to raise both her granddaughter and Sandra's one-year-old child."

Cases of sexual abuse represent a very small percentage of cases that child protective services deals with, yet because of the shame still attached to such behaviors, we can't say we have accurate numbers. From an ACE survey that included 10 states and Washington DC, 15 percent of women and 6 percent of men reported past sexual abuse. Surveys of adult women have indicated that sexual violence is something that impacts one out of five girls and women, with perpetrators ranging from family members, friends of parents or once-trusted dating partners.

FOUR: *Did you often or very often feel that no one in your family loved you or thought you were important or special, or that your family didn't look out for each other, feel close to each other, or support each other?*

The goal of this question is to tease out when feelings of parental rejection were significant and emotionally unsettling over an extended period of time, which is emotional neglect and can be debilitating. Kids who don't feel close to or loved by their families, especially their parents, are locked up in a kind of emotional solitary confinement. Some manage to brush it off, while others are driven toward suicide, and everything in between. In some cases, emotional neglect alone can be so extreme that it leads the government to remove kids from their parent's homes.

Trina, a counselor in a rural community, told us about how many neglectful parents love their children and don't realize how their child could possibly feel unloved. One of her clients, who had a problematic past with substance abuse, tearfully realized this in a counseling session: "I tried to protect them from my substance use. I never used around them. [But] even though I wasn't using in front of them, I can only imagine how alone and unloved they felt being by themselves all the time." Even the behaviors of well-intentioned parents may unintentionally lead their children to feel unloved.

FIVE: *Did you often or very often feel that you didn't have enough to eat, had to wear dirty clothes, or had no one to protect you? Or your parents were too drunk or high to take care of you or take you to the doctor if you needed to go?*

This question deals with child neglect, which actually represents a vast majority of cases in the child welfare system. Sexual abuse is dramatic, and emotional abuse generates controversy because it's invisible and a lot of people think it's normal, so both get a great deal of attention while only representing a relatively small percentage of the child welfare caseload. But most neglect involves parents who don't have their lives together enough to provide the basics for their kids, either for lack of money, preoccupation with addiction, or some other tragic reason.

Neglect, in its various forms, can be traumatic in and of itself, but it also generates a host of immediate practical problems. Not having anything to eat at home, for instance, can leave more emotional scars that stay with kids throughout life and affect health and relationships, but they also leave kids hungry right now. Kids who are hungry certainly have a hard time paying attention in school, if they make it to school at all, leading to a host of other problems. And not making it to doctor or dentist appointments, of course, can threaten health and life.

Often, the neglect isn't even malicious. Carrie, a Child Protective Services investigator, once told a client, Jolee, that she needed to fix a hole in her floor that was big enough for her infant to fall through. A few days later, she ran into Jolee, walking on the side of the road with an armful of lumber for the repairs. "Jolee, did you leave your baby alone while you got your wood?" Carrie asked. "Yes, she's fine in her crib," Jolee said matter-of-factly, "she's too little to go anywhere."

This is all in a day's work for a CPS investigator: Sometimes, you get to teach a new parent that it's not okay to leave an infant alone for hours.

But these cases can be even more surreal. While Jolee's case involved dire poverty, a CPS worker named Scott once dealt with a neglect case involving an affluent family and their daughter, Tina, who had recently been checked into the hospital for malnutrition. After further investigation, it came out that Tina's mother was convinced that her daughter was allergic to everything except specially concocted shakes. The family had taken Tina to see numerous specialists, who had duly reported that no, she was not allergic to everything, but the mother just didn't buy it. The lack of acceptance of science-based explanations, Scott suspected, was related to some unusually fundamentalist religious convictions. Tina was placed in foster care, where she happily ate everything put in front of her without any allergy problems.

With this question and responses, CPS workers face a significant challenge: It's not against the law to be poor or to have problems keeping the logistics of your life together. Yet it causes problems we can't ignore. We've all seen, for example, reports that children actually go hungry sometimes in America. Surely not, we think, given food stamps and food banks, and that is a fair point. But those services are contingent on a parent having their act together enough to get themselves to the pickup point, and cuts to these services are proposed all the time. So yes, we have laws on the books that will take children from their parents for neglect of the basics (hygiene, shelter, and food) if it presents an immediate risk of serious harm. But our system doesn't always ensure that our most vulnerable populations can get at those basics.

SIX: *Did you live with anyone who was a problem drinker or alcoholic? Or who used street drugs?*

Drug and alcohol use is another big spectrum, but the key with this question is to focus on the word "problem." Do that, and we'll avoid a lot of useless chatter about whether watching your parents have a glass of wine with dinner is an adverse childhood experience. The goal is to figure out if parents are actually putting their children at risk with their use of drugs or alcohol (including prescription opioids), as in a case reported to us by David, a Child Protective Services social worker.

"We have a mother in our caseload that had had four drug-addicted babies in four years," David told us. "She repeatedly refuses family planning services."

Knowing that a hospital delivery would attract the attention of Child Protective Services, the mother gave birth to her most recent child at home, then waited four days for the drugs to clear the baby's system before bringing it in for the usual medical assessments, all the while continuing to use methamphetamine.

SEVEN: *Was your parent or stepparent often or very often pushed, grabbed, slapped, or hit by a thrown object? Or sometimes, often, or very often, kicked, bitten, hit with a fist, or hit with something hard? Or ever repeatedly hit for at least a few minutes or threatened with a gun or knife?*

As with other questions, the aim here isn't to establish a journalistic or documentary account of what happened, but rather to identify what a child saw. Child witnesses to domestic violence can suffer emotional trauma of varying degrees and may require trauma-informed mental health care after the fact.

Clients are full of heartbreaking stories, said Alexandra, a counselor at a community health center. "One of the striking consequences of domestic violence is the lasting effects on the children who grow up in these households, walking on eggshells and fearful of conflict through their adulthood. Often this affects their own ability to have intimacy in relationships with friends and romantic partners."

As discussed earlier with question two, controlling and violent behaviors exist on a continuum in many families. It's not uncommon for parents to look back on their childhoods and see some conflict between parents while failing to analyze the impact living with such conflict for years can have. It's like the classic example of the frog in the pot of water being brought to a boil. While few die from living in a household where domestic violence occurs, the incremental increase of stress can lead to trauma.

EIGHT: *Was a household member depressed or mentally ill? Or did a household member attempt suicide?*

Growing up in a household with a person suffering from untreated mental illness can be emotionally traumatic, and this question's continuum covers everything from someone being depressed for a short period of time to a parent who says, on a weekly basis, "If you don't come straight home from school I will kill myself."

"For children who grow up with a household member who has untreated (or in some cases treated) behavioral health issues, there is a sense of never knowing who you are coming home to," says Lilli, a counselor at a school-based health center. "As adults, these children may still struggle with attachment, post-traumatic stress, or the inability to trust that any relationship can be stable."

Gathering data on the percentage of parents with mental health challenges is not easy, but we can pull together enough data from different sources to safely conclude that children who grow up in households where parents struggle with untreated or misdiagnosed mental illness can expect serious adversity down the road.

NINE: *Were your parents separated or divorced?*

Divorce is pretty common and widely accepted as normal, and in some cases, may not cause much long-lasting trauma at all. The general civility of the parents and age of the children are just a couple of factors to consider. Sometimes, however, things can get ugly and leave lasting marks. This question aims to find out where people are at in terms of loss, guilt, or abject fear, because even in relatively ideal circumstances, divorce can be tough on kids for a long time.

"Many of my children clients come into counseling without the words to describe the pain they feel from their parents' divorce," says Amanda, a counselor at a community health center. "One client, a 14-year old boy, started telling me about dinner with his father. He said, in a very matter-a-fact way: 'Dad says I get to stay the weekend because mom cares more about her boyfriend than me.' This young man was conflicted, confused and anxious when his parents would make these slights towards one another. He felt close to and loved by both his dad and mom, but these comments impacted his ability to trust his feelings and created uncertainty of whom to believe."

But problems surrounding divorce extend beyond the emotional. For low income and even middle class parents it can be an express train to poverty. Throw in poor parental coping strategies, mental illness, or perhaps some substance abuse, and kids can end up homeless.

TEN: *Did a household member go to prison?*

Just like divorce, a household member going to prison can impact children in a variety of ways, and produce a wide variety of emotional reactions. A family member in prison might mean extreme financial hardship. It could trigger fresh strife in a family well accustomed to it. Children whose parents have been incarcerated may also have higher rates of a slew of mental and physical health problems.

"I had a mother and son in family counseling discussing the mother's time in prison," Erica, a community health center counselor, told us. "She was tearfully expressing her guilt and her son was comforting her. He, in his nine years of wisdom, said, "Mom, I am the man of the house and I am here to take care of you.' This as an example of how, when parents are in prison, children often lose out on their childhood, not only taking on adult roles but also interrupting or delaying development of social skills and enjoyment of childhood without adult responsibilities."

United States of trauma

The ACE Survey has been used in many states, and to nobody's surprise, we find significant parts of the population likely suffering some sort of trauma after enduring one or more adverse childhood experiences. Again, the more ACEs people have, the more negative health and wellbeing outcomes we can expect. And people have a lot. In the initial ACEs study, 37 percent of participants reported at least two ACEs. That's more than one third of America, likely experiencing a plethora of serious problems as adults because of their childhood experiences.

We have five individual states represented on the chart that follows, with data from the Behavioral Risk Factor Surveillance System (BRFSS) study conducted in 2009. Although New Mexico, Arkansas, Louisiana, Tennessee and Washington are quite different in terms of total population, demographics, and types of ACEs reported, we still see significant populations in all five reporting multiple ACEs. It's safe to say that these patterns apply to the rest of the country.

The data bring up questions that need answers: What percentage of those who reported more than one ACE sought mental health care and engaged in trauma-informed counseling? How many of those reporting ACEs would acknowledge that their children also experienced ACEs? Why might states differ and what can we learn from those with the lowest reported ACEs? If we drilled down deeper into the numbers, would we find that certain populations or geographical areas are more at risk for ACEs? Would we then be able to target our efforts at prevention and treatment of those populations?

	Survey Pop.	0 ACEs	1 ACE	2 ACEs	3 ACEs	4 ACEs	5 or more ACEs
Arkansas	3,558	46.9	21.0	11.2	7.1	5.9	8.0
Louisiana	8,147	42.6	24.7	12.9	7.7	5.5	6.6
New Mexico	5,271	39.0	21.8	12.6	10.1	7.1	9.5
Tennessee	2,327	43.5	20.8	12.6	8.3	6.2	8.7
Washington	6,926	34.6	23.0	14.6	10.3	7.5	10.1

NOTE: Percentages might not total to 100% because of rounding.

The answer to that last question is yes. Once again, the solutions can often be found in the data. What might be going on in states that keeps their residents away from ACEs? Is there a connection between low rates and the easy availability of preschool and youth mentoring? Do they have readily available physical and behavioral health care? A little digging into the states that are doing well might help us find ways to help those states that are struggling.

The first steps

We could obviously attempt to break down the data further (and we will later), but for the time being, let this sink in: There's a good chance you live in a state where a solid majority of your fellow residents have had at least one ACE. And while that can be brushed off (unfairly, we argue) as perhaps just a divorce or a parent who had a "minor" drinking problem (if there is such a thing), consider this: About one fifth to one quarter of your fellow state residents likely had two or three. Go ahead and survey the list of ACEs again, and see if you can pick out three that wouldn't, taken together, leave a bad mark. It's easy to see how some people might be able to at least cope with three, given the right help, but it's just as easy to imagine how it might nudge others into academic failure, destructive relationships, substance misuse, and an inability to hold down a steady job – to say nothing of being set up to repeat the cycle generation after generation.

And if that hasn't gotten uncomfortable enough, consider that the rate of people with four or more ACEs is in the mid-to-high teens. Project that percentage over just the state of California, and we're looking at 6.6 million people, roughly the population of the entire San Francisco Bay Area. They are all at grave risk to themselves and to others, and there are way too many of them to hide from.

Outrage would be an entirely appropriate response to this data assessment of the United States' childhood trauma problem, and we hope we've provoked a healthy portion of it in these pages already. But if we've learned anything from Anna's case, it's that this alone won't be enough. As a society, we're already pretty good at outrage, and have it honed to an algorithmic science courtesy of social media. It becomes part of a soothing ritual we perform after a tragedy, the last step of which is a return to a serene ignorance.

This is not something we can afford, so what does real action against this problem look like? First, don't assume that your local or state governments are on this. Nor can you safely assume that local "ACEs prevention projects" hosted by nonprofit agencies are actually engaged in data-driven work, at least not yet. Some agencies are doing the incredibly important and long term work of increasing access to school-based trauma informed care. (We salute them.) Other groups are still only facilitating fourth grade student workshops on sharing feelings, praying that increasing the knowledge of children will somehow decrease their parent's behaviors leading to trauma and maltreatment. (It won't.) Some good-hearted and well-intentioned people may participate in some interesting panel discussions at health conferences, organize a speaker's bureau or otherwise nibble around the edges, but it's not likely that anything strategic or system-wide is in the works in your area. The "plan" may well look like one full-time public health worker designated as the official state ACEs coordinator, without a budget or staff. This person won't be doing data-driven systems change work nor even be able to advocate for it (lest he or she break the unspoken rule of many government agencies that thou shalt stay out of the news media). It may fall to you and what friends and co-workers you can bring together to push your community and workplace toward even the first step of acknowledging the problem. Every town needs to draw a metaphorical line in the sand and say, "no more," but the first step of that journey requires lots of people simply knowing the problem exists.

DOM'S JOURNAL

We know all this talk of "awareness" seems pretty small ball – almost cliché, but we promise that a few informal conversations and a brief internet search of who is working on ACEs in your town is a good first step toward making other people care – especially lawmakers and those leading our major government agencies tasked with the health and safety of our kids.

During the AIDS epidemic, many years passed before governors or a president started talking about it. It was an uncomfortable issue and they probably would have rather avoided it. People in communities played nice at first, asking for help from city leaders, and later played hardball, protesting loudly and relentlessly at city halls and federal buildings. We can and must do the same. ACEs won't go away by being polite or even reasonable. I remember one AIDS protest in San Francisco at a federal building where hundreds of people wore yellow gloves covered in red paint. The color of blood was not lost on the police, nor government officials, as there was no cure for AIDS then, nor an HIV test. Infection was real.

Demonstrations were weekly back then, small and large. Silence = Death posters were all over the place. I have to won-der: will it take confrontational strategies, demonstrations, and in-your-face messaging on the streets and online to get our lawmakers to address this epidemic of childhood trauma? I know that we need to be careful comparing AIDS to ACEs – I do so with trepidation. Yet there's a sense of real urgency. Democracies don't run on autopilot, and the politicians that lead efforts to change are most likely counting on the unrelenting activism of people like you.

Chapter Four

_____

Our inheritance of horrors: The complex, chaotic, and invisible root causes of childhood trauma

Anna's Story

The story of Anna would not leave the state's media machine. The background of her mother, Cassandra, was examined from every angle. A stream of lurid tales emerged. But what the news media did not focus on was how Cassandra, and people like her, was set up from birth to fail as a mother. Nor was there detailed examination of the systemic problems within child welfare that would require a huge commitment on the part of the governor and lawmakers to fund real, sustainable, and effective change. Had there been more digging, it might have been discovered that Cassandra herself grew up in a violent household, ran away from home at age 14, began a serious meth habit, got pregnant at age 17, and again at age 19, lost custody of those two children in a different state prior to becoming pregnant at age 24 with Anna. Such a scenario would surprise nobody in the child welfare profession. If systems had been different, perhaps Cassandra would have received mental health care as a teenager and many of these problems could have been avoided entirely.

HOW CAN WE CONFRONT destructive habits as old as time?

By way of answering that, let's start with a critical question about bad coffee at the office: Why does it exist? Seriously, we want to know.

We run a Data Leaders and quality improvement program for child welfare professionals that teaches the fine art of collecting data and other information and using it to make a difference in their jobs – and thus, the lives of kids. But we always start with this coffee conundrum as a bit of an icebreaking exercise. It's one of those group brainstorms where people shout stuff out and we jot it down on a big piece of butcher paper.

The answers usually come quickly: Someone brought bad coffee. The machine doesn't work. The water is bad. The cups aren't cleaned properly. The person in charge of buying coffee only drinks tea and doesn't know anything about coffee.

We're just trying to have a bit of fun, of course, but the overall goal is serious. What we're doing here is a root cause analysis, something you'd expect to be part and parcel of every action taken by critical parts of government (but you'd be wrong). Root cause analysis is an essential part of solving any problem – even bad coffee – but it is often overlooked.

Our problem here is adverse childhood experiences, and the many rippling problems they cause in turn. So what are the root causes? How is it that humanity, which depends so much on harmonious group efforts to make up for the reality that we're not the fastest, biggest, or toughest animals on the planet, somehow puts up with and even adapts to practices that seem to stand in the way of progress? How does a species that thrives on all things social tolerate practices that make it hard to get along with each other? What's really behind this epidemic, and what factors do we need to consider (not actually solve quite yet) in order to plan our way out of it?

Root Cause One: A long history of violence

Not long ago, we came across a horrible crime story in a magazine. Some poor guy had his skull bashed in and was then summarily dumped in a cave. Does that sound familiar? Maybe something similar happened in the mountains near your town?

Actually, it's a trick question: We're really talking about the world's oldest known murder victim, a case that's 430,000 years old. Our source was National Geographic, but it could have been in your local paper, and that's the point.

We've been at this violence thing for a long time. So have our closest primate cousins: In the 1970s, Jane Goodall famously documented a four-year war between factions of chimpanzees that featured all kinds of murder and mayhem. Suffice it to say that if you were to put a random human from four thousand years ago into a time machine and transport them to the present day, they would likely be amazed by our touchscreens and Skype and limitless food supplies. But the only thing that would strike them as abnormal about the Rwandan genocide would be the slickly manufactured stainless steel machetes.

Sometimes, violence is domestic. Sometimes, it's between two people or two clans. Sometimes, it is institutionalized into slavery or the subjugation of women. Sometimes, it may not even look violent to the untrained eye. But if whatever order we're talking about is backed up by threats and intimidation, it's violence.

We'll leave it to the evolutionary biologists to decide why violence is so prominent. Presumably, it helped our ancestors survive long enough to reproduce more than it hurt. Suffice it to say that it has been a very big deal for a very long time, and it is most likely to impact the weakest members of society, especially children. There is some evidence to suggest that we're actually living in the least violent era of human history, but old habits die hard.

Root Cause Two: Mental illness

We'll devote an entire chapter to this topic, but for now let's just stipulate that mental health care and mental health awareness are in a dreadful state. We'll automatically tell someone with a broken leg to go to the hospital, but we're terrible at recognizing a need for mental health care in ourselves and others. A strong undercurrent of society seems to believe that mental illness is not really a thing or that it shows weakness or some other stigmatized state of being. And often the people who need it the most are the same people who have a lot of trouble functioning in our modern economy, which is a fancy way of saying they're poor and can't afford it. With the health insurance mess at various stages of dysfunction across 50 states, even middle class folks struggle to afford long term counseling. Public programs created to make sure poor people have health care are generally underfunded, which means there are shortages of providers.

Oh, and one more thing: Just like with violence, the situation is grim, but it is also the best it has ever been. An overwhelming majority of human history was much worse than this. Root cause indeed.

Root Cause Three: The poor have always been with us

Poverty has always been a feature of human life, and a risk factor of childhood trauma. Poverty can be the symptom of some other problem, like a mental illness that makes it hard to earn money. But it can also be the disease: Lack of money can make it hard to feed your kids, it can end marriages, and it can drive you to drink or do drugs, which drives you to prison, and we've just covered four of the ten ACEs.

But it was much worse in times gone by. About 20 percent of the world lives in extreme poverty today, but that number was at 40 percent in 1990, and close to 100 percent a century before that. Stressful hand-to-mouth existences were completely normal for most of human history, and this likely didn't do much to promote peaceful human relations or discourage child neglect. We're doing relatively well on this front in the United States, though we still have dire poverty in many areas, and even some pockets of extreme poverty, which is defined as living on $2 per day or less. Much of the rest of the world, of course, is even less lucky.

Root Cause Four: We abuse and misuse substances

Addiction can lead to violence, and we humans have been abusing substances for a long time. Alcoholism even comes up in the Bible, and some scientists argue that the reason we quit being hunter-gatherers in the first place was to make it easier to grow grain for beer. It probably helped foster a sense of community, but the downside was very real.

Root Cause Five: We're too adaptable for our own good

However our parents raise us, we tend to think of it as perfectly normal and perfectly healthy. And since we tend to think highly of ourselves, we're also capable of dismissing all manner of unhealthy behavior inflicted on us ("I got beat as a kid, but I turned out fine..."). Today and in the Bronze Age, we are still social creatures, and if the inputs are bad, the outputs will probably be bad, yet this does not often prevent passing them to the next generation. Evolution doesn't require perfection. It requires being good enough to make copies.

Speaking of making copies...

Root Cause Six: Teens without resources having children

The teen pregnancy rate in the United States has steadily declined for the last few decades. However, we still have a substantially higher rate than other industrialized nations. No matter your opinion on birth control, the social and economic costs of teen pregnancy are huge. Children of low-income teen moms are more likely to drop out of high school, have health problems, get incarcerated, and continue the cycle as teen parents. (Sounds kind of like an ACE doesn't it?). All of these add up to significant costs to you, John Q. Taxpayer.

Those who live in the least favorable socioeconomic conditions, meanwhile, are the most likely to become teenage parents. And guess who is at the highest risk: the very kids we are trying to protect. Children in foster care are more than twice as likely to become pregnant as those who aren't.

Root Cause Seven: Weak extended families

The old saw about a village being necessary to raise a child is true. When kids have access to a healthy network of adults who are not their parents, they tend to be more well-adjusted and well-rounded. They end up with more job connections and opportunities for healthy and enriching recreation. Parents who have access to this network get more support as well: They have shoulders to cry on, experts to compare notes with, access to perfectly good clothes other kids have grown out of, and an informal mutual aid babysitting society.

This is the one rare area where pre-modern humans might have had a leg up on the modern world: They lived in close quarters, often with three or four generations under the same roof, and there may well have been other parental surrogates around to offer advice and model better alternatives. Single moms were not isolated – just absorbed into the group, and parenting was more of a collective enterprise.

We're not saying that living in extended family units prevents ACEs, but it seems reasonable to assume that kids have a better chance when they are being monitored by more than one pair of eyes.

Root Cause Eight: These days, we're more individualistic than communitarian

Maybe blame it on our wealth. The middle and upper classes can move all the time, which weakens ties to extended families and means we arrive in big new cities with few friends. There seems to be a correlation between money and wholesale rejection of religion, one historically popular source of community. We don't have that many kids, so family reunions can fit in small apartments. (In lots of cultures past and present, family reunions would be a hopelessly silly idea, since they happen all the time in the normal course of living life.) And we're incredibly diverse, which according to some evidence reduces social trust. Plus, the pursuit of happiness is something of a national religion, but doesn't really strike the ear as something you do in a big group.

This all serves as a drag on progress in the child welfare field. Simply put, doing something to help the kids requires spending time and money on people you don't know who often don't look like you. There's still a good argument that doing so is in your self-interest, but it makes for a harder sell. Good kids are raised in communities, but when proposals come up to make the broader society more like an extended family, the first political instinct of conservatives and not a few liberals is to say, "not my kid, not my problem."

It doesn't have to be this way, of course. First, let's take a predictable example from a generous European welfare state. Sweden operates on an "everybody in, nobody out" sort of social welfare model. The government makes sure that all citizens have access to basic services, regardless of ability to pay. There's universal health care, parental leave, generous welfare and unemployment benefits, and all kinds of other supports.

And their success is obvious: Four percent of Swedish women have a baby before age 20, but that figure is 22 percent in the United States. The country has one of the highest life expectancies in the world, and can frequently be found at the top of "quality of life" or "best countries" lists.

But this is not a phenomenon confined to the sort of European countries that liberals like to wistfully cite in books about the problems that kids face. You can also see it in deep red Utah, where the Church of Jesus Christ of Latter-Day Saints operates a parallel welfare system that works hand in glove with the state, something that seems to dampen the usual opposition to social programs. The religion mandates tithing to support all this, and generally makes a big deal about helping the less fortunate.

Beyond that, the Mormons tend to emphasize community and supportive families more than most religions. Official church functions are suspended every Monday to encourage Family Home Evening, a weekly tradition where families spend time together in a combination of religious education and activities like board games. The definition of "family" is pretty liberal as well, and young single Mormons living away from home also have opportunities to join families of peers.

The results are equally impressive: The state has some of the best upward mobility rates in the nation. Salt Lake City also managed to all-but-eliminate chronic homelessness.

Root Cause Nine: Child Welfare only recently became a thing

The idea that child welfare could be a driving force behind formal organizations is just over 100 years old, a mere eye blink in the sweep of human history. In The New Yorker, in 2016, Jill Lepore wrote about one of the first high profile cases that spurred more organized action:

In New York in 1874, the Times reported that a girl named Mary Ellen Wilson was "rescued" from her home by a charity worker whose husband happened to be a newspaper reporter. The rescue was made possible with the help of the Society for the Prevention of Cruelty to Animals. This and other cases led to the founding of the Society for the Prevention of Cruelty to Children. It did for children what its sister organization did for animals. "Lists of 'saved children' joined those kept for 'redeemed dogs,'" [Historian] Judith Sealander ... argues that the dead-baby story proved so successful because infant and childhood mortality was falling, fast. "Before the early nineteenth century, the average child was the dead child," Sealander writes. "For most of human history, probably seven out of ten children did not live past the age of three."

Let's for a moment try to tamp down whatever personal rage we may feel about a society for the prevention of animal cruelty predating one for the prevention of cruelty to children. Big groups of people came together with the simple mandate of finding hurting kids and doing something about it, and that was excellent progress. Voluntary organizations like it spread through the country, with members intervening on behalf of children however they could, and that was the system for many decades, for better or worse. As you might expect, these small societies didn't have the capacity to do a comprehensive job and didn't cover rural areas very well, so eventually states moved to put child protection in government hands, something they fully accomplished only in the 1960s.

That may still seem like enough time to have figured it out, but sadly, we think it's not. It's a much more complex problem than, say, building and maintaining roads. There's lots of coordination to be done with various other government entities, which is never easy. Drug epidemics and economic fluctuations can dramatically change the nature of the challenge in a way that is wholly unlike the problems confronted by the state parks department. And the departments themselves are often as neglected by state governments as the children they seem to help.

Is it lame to say a 50-year-old bureaucracy is still learning as they go? Yes, but it's also true. They're big sprawling organizations, and while they're better than voluntary societies, they're still subject to turf wars, siloed thinking, bad coordination, and good hard-working people who are nonetheless not listened to by higher ups who, in some states, value hunches over actual evidence.

Root Cause Ten: Humans are not good at problems like this

Obviously, what we need here is a highly coordinated, flexible, and innovative response that evolves on the fly, the better to help all our kids. This, however, is easier said than done. Frankly, humans are pretty terrible at doing stuff like that, especially when acting through their governments, and that's one reason we didn't solve it hundreds of years ago and still haven't today.

Under an obvious, tangible, understandable threat, we'll quickly unify, rally around our leaders, and do what we can to kill the leopards or defeat the Axis powers or put up a shelter for the victims of the flood. We're really good at that, and we absolutely love doing it. When temperatures get dangerously cold, we put all hands on deck to get the homeless off the streets. When disaster strikes, we rush to the scene and help, and those that don't happily open their wallets and organize benefit concerts.

But that's the easy part. What do we do for the homeless the rest of the year, when it's cold but not "killer cold?" Not much. And what do we do to make sure the levy that would prevent that disaster is in good working order? (Ask New Orleans.) For that matter, what do we do about a climate problem that makes nasty storms more common? Again, not much. Those are the complex, sometimes invisible problems that require a lot of forward thinking and coordination, and lack a definitive and impactful end point. Those are the kind of counterintuitive, slow-moving problems we're not good at.

Eastman Kodak saw digital cameras coming, but failed to adapt. Sears saw Amazon coming, but failed to adapt. And although you can doubtless see old age coming, you probably don't have enough saved for your retirement.

Governments are no different. They're pretty good at doing simple, repetitive tasks with highly visible and obvious metrics for success. Every day, we entrust the postal service with personal letters, important legal communication, and unfathomably large checks, and by and large, those items get to their destination without undue delay, all for some of the lowest postage rates in the developed world. The post office keeps doing the same thing over and over, and despite the occasional griping about lines, we keep on using it, because it's efficient and reliable. Meanwhile, we can sign up for an immensely complex health insurance plan on healthcare.gov in an hour or two, and even arrange for elaborate financial aid right there. And when the military puts its mind to it, it can depose whatever foreign regime happens to be on the president's bad side.

These are all immensely complex tasks, to be sure, but the overall goal is simple and so acts as a powerful organizer. Get this letter from Point A to Point B. Match an American citizen with an insurance company. Kill the guy in the palace. We've done it all before, we know how to do it again, and we all know what victory looks like. There's not much to argue about.

But ask those same organizations to innovate, do counter-intuitive things, and evolve with changing circumstances, and things get hairy pretty fast. The post office has been trying to figure out how to adapt to lower volumes of mail for many years now, but the various unions and political overseers have been fighting about how to do that, so the core problem remains unsolved. The military efficiently toppled the Iraqi government, but had a much harder time getting a highly sectarian country (with few civil society groups or democratic norms) to come together after the fact. And while healthcare.gov presently runs pretty well, we all remember the chaotic launch.

From root causes to a plan: Why sunlight is the best disinfectant

We have the data to show that we all pay through the nose for childhood trauma, whether it's in the form of a high ACEs score in our own past, a larger tax bill, or diminished quality of life. With a mastery of all media, including traditional TV, radio, and outdoor advertising, plus social media, we can spread this message and educate people, just like we do with drug abuse, recycling, and the more effective political campaigns. Efforts on Twitter and Instagram and Facebook, coupled with the popularity and effectiveness of short video and infographics, can tell this story in surprisingly detailed and provocative ways.

But that's old news: We already knew that we could get a message through with the proper organizing. It's just a matter of skillfully connecting the dots and pushing the technology to its full potential. The question is what people will do with the information. With lots of problems, we know that a message of "please care, because this situation is awful" doesn't work very well. But the message here is "please care, because it's a direct threat to you and your money," and we like our chances with that.

We need only look at the reaction to Zika and the Ebola virus to find reason for optimism. Both generated immense global concern and some mustering of resources against the problem. But why? Out of concern for the poor Bolivians or Liberians? Not a chance. We cared that much because we were afraid that Zika would go from being a problem in Santa Cruz, Bolivia to being a problem in Santa Cruz, California. We sympathized with the poor residents of Monrovia,

Liberia during the Ebola outbreak, of course, but the reason we happily poured resources into the country had more to do with not wanting to see the outbreak spread to Monroe County, Illinois.

Is that cynical? Maybe, but we don't care. Humans are more likely to take action when they perceive a threat. With childhood trauma, we now have the information to make that threat visible. If citizens and their media can get everyone to notice the anchor hanging on the necks of the comfortable, we're optimistic that we'll all end up doing something to help the afflicted.

———————————

An infant, a motel room, and a pile of needles: How we set up a vital institution to fail

Anna's Story

We all make mistakes, but when Child Protective Services makes a mistake it can cost a child's life. While very rare, child fatalities may be the direct cause of a staffer's misjudgment. It could be the result of missing or incomplete files, a case being transferred to other staff without sufficient briefings, or just having a very distracted week with a million other pressing tasks to finish. As former employees of child welfare operations, we have collaborated with some of the noblest, most hard-working colleagues we've ever encountered. But we also know that cases like Anna's, to varying degrees, happen all too frequently in all too many communities. And that troubles us deeply.

SUSAN WAS ASLEEP as the clock slouched toward 1 a.m., when the phone rang. The Child Protective Services statewide intake hotline center was on the other end, and they wanted her at a motel near the airport right away. Police had already arrived, and would be waiting for her.

As Susan turned into the parking lot, she noticed a squad car blocking an old van in its parking spot in front of a room. Outside, a mom we'll call Laura cried and spoke into a phone: "You got to come over now, Ed," she said. "Get the hell back here." She was slurring her words, thanks to some as-yet-unknown substance, or more likely, substances.

Inside the dingy motel room, a four-year-old girl named Jen sat on a chair, looking as though it was way past her bedtime. And in the bathroom, an infant we'll call Lizzy cried from a car seat, an array of syringes splayed around her on the floor.

Susan's job as a Child Protective Services investigator, at this hour so late it was almost early, was to determine, in consultation with the police, if the kids needed to go straight into protective custody, or to some family member. Ed turned out to be the father, but before too long it became obvious that he was not coming. Clearly, Laura was in no shape to parent at the moment.

Susan would spend the rest of the night and a good chunk of the morning trying to track down relatives, and after not finding a suitable one, contacting a list of over-worked, under-supported foster parents, all with the goal of finding a safe place for the kids to go. Thus began, for her, another day at the office.

So it goes every hour of every day and every night. As you read this, somewhere out there in America, there is something awful like this happening – some equivalent of Lizzy, in the car seat on the hotel bathroom floor, surrounded by syringes.

You don't need a license to have kids, and there's no authority that routinely checks up on people to make sure they're not botching the job spectacularly. But once in a while, things get so bad that we as a society decide it's time to intervene, and that intervention takes the form of sending people like Susan to dingy hotel rooms in the middle of the night. As we do with the cops, we scrape together a pile of intractable problems from society's most challenging corners, dump them into the lap of some bureaucrat, and say, "here, handle this." Meanwhile, the rest of us get off easy, raging as we do against irresponsible moms, deadbeat dads, drugs, or perhaps an entire ethnicity, then calling it a day.

Investigator Susan knows that rage will not actually find a permanent and safe home for the girls, so she must engage in a protracted investigation full of judgement calls, reports, and interviews that really comes down to a simple question: Will these kids live with their parents or not?

All things being equal, of course, kids are better off in the family home. The attachments we form to parents are powerful and rupturing them is all but guaranteed to bring with it major consequences. Kids taken away from their parents have all kinds of trouble relating to others – what we formally call emotional attachment – and those problems can continue for decades. This severely constrains their ability to build their own healthy families, make money, build social capital, and generally be happy.

Taking kids into custody, meanwhile, also causes them trauma. Foster homes are often in short supply, and group homes are a poor imitation of the family life that all kids need. The process, even with the most well-resourced child welfare system, adds a few straws to the camel's back of emotional health in already traumatized children.

Further complicating matters is the practical matter of the backlash that taking kids into custody can create. Parents tend to dislike it, to say the least, and are often happy to engage in a protracted legal fight to regain custody. It can cause political problems as well, depending on how well the parents know powerful people. And of course, taking kids into custody drives up the numbers of kids in custody, putting pressure on the already overburdened system and possibly attracting unwanted attention from politicians and other higher ups. So there are all kinds of reasons, good and bad, to keep kids where they are, however less-than-functional the situation might be.

But then there are the syringes on the bathroom floor – a powerful counter argument, to say the least. And the bottom line in decisions in child welfare is always physical safety first.

It is of course possible that Laura, the mom responsible for the dingy motel and the syringes, can be persuaded or cajoled into getting her act together. Maybe a little treatment, a little counseling, and the right parenting support will bring enough stability to raise a couple of kids well enough, and they can all live at least somewhat happily ever after. Or maybe it would work for a year or two, then fall apart in another motel room. Maybe next time, the kids wouldn't be lucky enough to live.

Only an omniscient deity would truly know the right strategy every time. But since none seems immediately willing to run the department, we ask people like Susan to make educated guesses, based on state and federal guidelines, about circumstances which neither she nor anyone can fully know, while the very lives of children hang in the balance. We ask her to assess which evil is lesser, and just how – not whether – kids should be put at further risk. There is no easy path for these children in the hotel room with syringes on the floor, and there is no easy path for Susan the investigator. While being taken away from their families may put children at a lower risk for physical harm, the emotional and well-being ramifications of putting a child into foster care are not trivial. At every step of this process, there is plenty of room for error, and if an error is big enough, there's a chance that the wrath of thousands could suddenly flow like water. Susan is an umpire, but this is not a game. And this is only one of 20 to 30 cases she is dealing with at any given moment.

Anatomy of a case: On the beat with a child welfare worker

NOTE: While federal guidelines set benchmarks and standards, all 50 state child welfare systems, and those run by counties, may operate slightly or dramatically differently. The scenarios highlighted in this chapter provide a general overview.

Meet Craig, a 32-year-old who works for Child Protective Services under the title "investigator." A few years ago, he graduated with a bachelor's degree in social work, a program that is part psychology, part sociology, part law, and part public policy. He works in a cubicle in a crowded office in a drab building, because state governments are always under enormous pressure to not spend ostentatiously. The building itself is not located in the worst part of town, but it's far from the relative glitz of downtown.

Elsewhere in Craig's mid-sized city, a school nurse is calling Child Protective Services to make a report about Polly, a third grader who appears malnourished and has unexplained bruises. That report is taken by a statewide central call center, then forwarded to Craig's boss, who forwards it to Craig. Craig receives it because he recently closed a case, and his total number now stands at 15, which is about ideal according to the Child Welfare League of America standard. Many of Craig's colleagues across the country, however, handle between 20 and 30.

Many cases that come through are repeats, but this one is new, so Craig doesn't have much to go on save the facts outlined above, and that means a thorough research project. This part of the job resembles some combination of journalist and cop on the beat. Craig will interview everyone concerned, generally at their homes. He will interview Polly, her siblings, her parents, parents' boyfriends and girlfriends, and any family members who could lend some perspective. He will talk to the school nurse as well, and probably Polly's teacher.

The presenting symptoms of bruises and perceived malnourishment could lead in several directions. The best-case scenario is a few rough outings on the playground that Polly didn't want to talk about for some innocent reason, plus an undiagnosed case of anemia. One worst case scenario is a parent with a mental health problem leading her to believe that Polly is not deserving of food but is still deserving of routine physical abuse. And of course, it's possible that there is a whole mess of undiscovered problems that threaten Polly, just waiting for someone like Craig to start asking questions.

Many other scenarios could play out between those two extremes. The bruises may be innocently acquired, but the mental health and food deprivation is real. Maybe the anemia is real and so is the physical abuse. Maybe the malnourishment is real, but the result of a simple failure to apply for food stamps. Maybe Polly's parents are afraid to apply because they have an undocumented grandparent living with them and don't want to go anywhere near the government. Or maybe they're busy pursuing various addictions and a life of crime. Craig's job is to figure out where on this spectrum between innocent enough and pernicious this case's reality happens to land.

As it happens, the bruises do not appear to be connected with physical abuse, but Polly is not getting enough to eat because her mother, Jane, won't feed her properly, fearing she will get fat. It also turned out that on a few occasions, Jane locked Polly in a closet for several hours as punishment for eating candy.

The situation is bad, but perhaps repairable. Craig collects all the information from interviews, writes everything up, recommends that Polly be taken into protective custody, and presents these findings to a family court judge, who orders Polly's removal from the home. The social workers and their clients may be the focus of the child welfare narrative, but everything actually takes place under the umbrella of a judicial proceeding. The state is essentially suing Polly's mom, who, along with attorneys (usually court-appointed), will enter into a formal dispute resolution process supervised by a judge.

Order in hand, Craig and a colleague or two will show up with law enforcement at Polly's house and take her away. Parents are typically caught off guard by this, despite having been interviewed and knowing this was a possibility, and they may yell, scream, cry, and hurl all kinds of verbal abuse at people like Craig. Even the least capable parents are generally distraught about the government coming to take their kids away.

Polly will probably cry through the whole experience as well, as she is transported to a foster home, where stable adults who are trained at foster parenting and have passed a background check are ready to feed her properly and make sure she is safe. The social worker will try to comfort her, maybe provide her with a backpack or some fresh clothes. Although very rare these days, in less ideal circumstances, Polly might end up in a group home, a kind of dormitory for kids with nowhere else to go that is about as not-family-like as it sounds.

The process is just beginning. Jane, Polly's mom, will soon appear in family court, where Craig and the judge will lay out exactly what needs to happen if Polly is to come back to her. Because Jane has some seriously irrational ideas about proper diet, the court will probably force her to undergo a mental health evaluation. If that evaluation unearths a chronic disconnection from reality, that may be the end of Jane's chances to regain custody – at least for a while. But luckily for Jane (and we hope luckily for Polly) the aversion to feeding her daughter, upon further investigation, turned out to be a combination of ignorance and obsessive-compulsive disorder. The judge ordered regular visits to a therapist, and Jane cooperated. By this time, Polly has been in custody for a week.

We throw words like "treatment" and "professional help" around quite a bit, but those big words may obscure a simpler reality: Jane had some bizarre ideas about nutrition, and her mental health condition seemed to solidify them. She needed to sit down with someone well versed in the study of human behavior and be subjected to a process of being talked out of it, with Jane herself doing most of the talking. Craig made sure she got a first appointment and kept going back.

Meanwhile, the case gets transferred over to Liza, a "permanency worker" with a portfolio that is often mistaken for "social worker." Essentially, that means Craig will be handing this case to a colleague who specializes not in investigations, but finding the safest permanent living situation for Polly. Liza is tasked with determining which option is best for the child: reuniting with her mom, or terminating her mom's parental rights and trying for adoption. The permanency worker will make "reasonable efforts" to keep Polly out of the adoption track by seeing to it that Jane gets the services and support that will help her become a better parent.

The permanency worker is also mindful of a national guideline that says this process should conclude, one way or another, in one year or less, if the goal is to get Polly home to her mom. The policy, written with the idea that we shouldn't jerk kids around a stressful legal process for their entire childhoods, essentially tells child welfare agencies and the parents they work with that the one year mark is the time to fish or cut bait. Jane has about that long to get it together, or the permanency worker can make Polly's custody permanent by petitioning the court to terminate parental rights and put her up for adoption, ideally with the foster family she has been staying with.

If Jane needs two years to get it together, she may be out of luck when it comes to regaining custody. But of course, this all depends on a number of factors, like the permanency worker's analysis of the case, the availability of foster parents, the politics of "clearing cases" as dictated by upper management, the quality of Jane's court appointed attorney, and the particular family court judge who hears the case.

The sooner children can achieve "permanency," the better chance they will have to build a family bond with their adoptive parents, something that's critical for more than the obvious emotional reasons. Most families, biological and adoptive, help their kids well into adulthood, with advice, support, job connections, a place to crash, and money, and this is enormously helpful for the younger generation. But when foster kids become adults (at age 21 in some states and age 18 in others), they are no longer in the state's custody. Most states have a unit designed to support the youth who are aging out of foster care, and help get them ready for adult life. But like most of their colleagues, youth transition workers are overworked, underpaid, and just have too much of a caseload to provide these youth with the support they need. Add a lifetime of trauma that most of the kids have been through, and needless to say, this does not often go well.

This massively complex and fast-moving target also explains why investigators and permanency workers should only have about 15 cases at any given time. One could make the rounds and meet with 15 people in a week, of course, but the job is much more complex than that. There are those other interviews to conduct, colleagues to consult with, and mountains of paperwork. Each interview must be documented, each court appearance prepared for, and little details followed up upon. Multiply that by 15, and child workers like Craig are very busy people. Complicating the issues is that some cases involve a mom and a daughter while others involved extended family members and many children – perhaps a dozen people in all. This means workloads and caseloads have to be looked at closely if one wants an effective child protective services system.

It took a few months, but Jane managed to make enough progress to convince Liza and the judge that if Polly were returned, she would not starve. A gavel came down, an order was signed, Polly moved back home, and Liza moved on to the rest of her docket.

How it all goes wrong

That is of course, how it is all supposed to work in an ideal world. Liza and Craig (ever the dedicated public servants) work had, are not yet burned out, and Jane has only one big problem that, happily enough, is treatable. While it's a useful illustration, in reality the child welfare system is much more complicated.

In more common scenarios, stressed out investigators work with lousy equipment under shaky processes in long-forgotten corners of state government, and only get noticed when one of the cases they're managing blows up.

Problems can crop up from the very beginning, with the immensely complex machine known as reporting. It's easy enough for a civilian to phone in a report to child protective services, and if you don't have the number, the cops certainly do, but what happens after that information is taken down? Lots of things, some of which are bad. The report could stall out in a computer system, without any action, simply because the person who answered the phone that day didn't think it quite merited action. There may be a procedure to thoroughly and expertly review all those calls, but in some jurisdictions, it might just be a slapdash affair.

So begins the invisibility of the child welfare system that all but guarantees its overwhelming dysfunction. If a couple of people started a knife fight outside the school nurse's house, the call to the police would provide an easily verifiable result. The police would either show up and deal with it, or the nurse's next call would be to the mayor's office demanding to know what we pay all these taxes for.

But when that same nurse calls a Child Protective Services hotline, that easy accountability becomes opaque. Depending on how the call was rated – priority one, two, or three – the investigator arrives to interview the child within hours or days or may even be delayed further. The nurse can't generally see the process at all.

Reports can also generate crushing caseloads for investigators like Craig. We gave him 15 cases in this story, which is ideal, but people like him routinely try to balance 30 cases or more. While most investigators could take on a few extra cases and make it work, doubling the ideal workload all but guarantees slow-motion failure.

We don't usually conceptualize child welfare work like this, but it's really just a long series of procedures and processes that could be illustrated in a flow chart. Task A must be completed by Deadline B so that Person C can do Thing D. When the workload reaches a frantic level, three things happen: First, things slow down, putting what should be a temporary situation into long-term limbo. Second, the cases that are on fire get all the attention. Third, all those parents, whose reform efforts are the most expendable part of a daily grind that includes innocent kids and no-nonsense judges, are left to fend for themselves.

If Polly's case had been Craig's 30th case, instead of his 15th, we could expect very different results. There would probably have been significant delays in the collection of all the information and the setting of a court date. The information collection might well have been less comprehensive. And instead of going the extra mile by making some phone calls to ensure that Jane got a behavioral health appointment, Craig likely would have spent the time putting out fires on the rest of his caseload or trying to document what he had done, because "if it's not documented, it didn't happen."

It all seems so bureaucratically mundane, but the delays mean that Polly would spend more time in foster care limbo, unsure if she would find a new permanent home or be sent back to her mom. Thin information collection means a process that already involves a fair amount of educated guessing would involve more guessing and less education, which is not ever ideal, especially when a kid's health or life is at stake. And it's easy to imagine how Craig's call to a behavioral health provider could have been that extra push that Jane needed.

It's an old story of bad inputs leading to bad outputs, but it's entirely possible that if Liza had 30 cases, Polly would have ended up further traumatized and in foster care for life, while leaving Jane to languish without the sort of help that could get her life back on track. Overtaxing the system, in other words, means more broken lives and fewer available foster parents.

A software versus people problem

There's a basic computer software problem at many child welfare departments as well, because the systems used to track through this maze of reports are often so antiquated (many are using the same systems that were developed in 1997) that it's difficult to call up information even after you've learned the overly complex rules. Like filing taxes, every problem usually has a solution, but it's so mind-numbingly complicated that it slows things down, adding time to Craig's day that should be spent helping kids. Computer systems are always a bit of a foreign language, but if we make it more like learning Pig Latin, rather than Mandarin, Craig can spend more time doing what we want him to do.

The complexity often extends to the rest of the group and how it collectively gets work done. Anyone running an organization, whether in the public or private sector, knows how important it is to have all employees on the same page, with a shared understanding of how a work process is supposed to happen, who does what, and what good project outcomes look like. Whether it's software development, or efforts to protect a child, a system should be clearly understood and transparent if it is going to function well.

In the process of running a program for a protective services agency, we once set about creating simple work flow diagrams that attempted to spell out that system simply and visually. But it took months, because every time we interviewed a manager or field worker about the process, they had a different perception of how things actually worked. We eventually created a document that management signed off on, but only after 20 revisions. We're aware that "getting the process right" may be the least interesting words ever committed to paper, but anything less represents a small but significant time tax on every hour of every day. And that tax is levied on staffers who have more important things to do, and ultimately on the children and families who need someone to help them.

And it probably goes without saying, but our favorite subject of using data to predict and prevent problems does not usually work its way into bureaucratic systems staffed by social workers with double the recommended caseload. That's a shame, for one simple and clichéd reason: If you can't measure it, you can't manage it.

We once worked for a child welfare department in a bureau dedicated to research, assessment, and data, which put us in a great position to have all the information about where our biggest challenges were. We could filter data by geographical characteristics and demographics, and we could figure out which regional offices were lagging behind. We had the information that could inform reform, but did not have the authority to enact it.

The conundrum was reinforced as we attended national conferences with our peer data nerds. Turned out that we were all in agreement about what we could see and what needed to be done, but we were not high enough in the agency pecking order to do anything about it. This led to some serious mental anguish for us and our colleagues across the nation. Do we speak up in management meetings and risk being labeled a 'troublemaker,' or do we remain silent and work in stealth among our peers?

Data-rich information pool

Child Protective Services doesn't usually think of itself as a data collection operation. In reality, they're swimming in it, but most don't use it to maximum effect. There's nothing in particular that stops them from looking at repeat maltreatment cases in an effort to find patterns and learn something about the risk factors that are most likely to lead to repeated foster care episodes. They could look at the length of time kids are spending in custody and probably learn something about how regional offices are performing and why. They could take the numbers of teens aging out of the system without a permanent arrangement and have a good idea of how the overall mission is going, or at the very least an idea of how the social fabric in a given state is holding up. And they could illustrate just how well parents are able to access the sort of mental health care and other supports that are most likely to help them get their kids back.

Take for example, using data to learn something about child welfare's efforts to retain and recruit foster parents. This sort of data-driven analysis might well lead them to stories like one faced by Paul, a corporate trainer we know who had been thinking about becoming a foster parent. Raised by a single mom, he knew well the difficulty of growing up without much in the way of male role models, and wanted to do something to help. But when he did a quick online search for foster parenting on his state's child welfare agency web site, he couldn't find anything about requirements or training.

Eventually, he found an email address, fired off a query about fostering, and waited to hear back. Many weeks passed until the response arrived, directing him back to the agency's web site, and the dates of an evening orientation. He also read on the site that he would have to commit to four Saturdays over two months for official and mandatory foster parent training. Undeterred but having questions, Paul emailed the representative back to see if he could arrange to speak with her. Another few weeks passed, and a call was finally booked. During the conversation, Paul learned that the course would involve reading a 130-page manual, but the official didn't have much information beyond that. There was nothing about what the four-part course would cover, or whom would be doing the instructing.

Paul, remember, did training for a living, and by now he was noticing a lot of red flags. He could just imagine some burned-out instructor, very unhappy about having to give up a weekend and making damn sure that everyone in the class would soon reach an equal level of non-happiness. And if learning about the process was this difficult, he figured, imagine how awful the actual fostering parent training and approval process would be.

Paul changed strategies, opting to give back through a youth mentoring agency instead, and so child welfare lost another potential asset as Big Brother Big Sisters gained one. Still, it's a near miracle that Paul got that far in the first place, given those obstacles.

It doesn't take a management consultant to know that the first step to solving a foster parent shortage is an intuitive, artfully-designed website and timely responses to emailed questions. Some states have figured it out, because they are using data to track the "user experiences" of everyone interacting with their agency, but many others have yet to get the memo (or collect and analyze the data). Often it's the states with the greatest need that lack the resources to provide good customer service. They don't have the staff or the right technology.

And then there is the usual stuff that you would expect from any government agency: Turf wars, internal politics, finger pointing, confusing signals from cabinet secretaries and governors, misread tea leaves, and contradictory mandates written from legislatures. But you'll find that at the department of transportation as well, yet they still manage to build some pretty impressive roads. You'll find that at fish and game too, but the rivers still get stocked and people still get busted for hunting elk out of season. Even tourism departments put out pretty slick and impressive commercials.

What's different about child welfare is that we can't see the outputs. Lay people can drive around town, take a few buses, check out some potholes, and have a pretty good idea of how transportation policy is going, but child welfare is not laid out like that for all to see. To be sure, there's a natural aversion to learning about the fates of society's most troubled, weakest members. There are today and will always be those who prefer to endlessly complain about what they see as "stupid poor people do stupid things to mess up their stupid lives," and we're just going to have to live with them. But for the people who care, if only a little, we must stop thinking that the enormity of challenges facing child welfare are just too complex, and that there's just no way to know if it's all working. That defeatist thinking has to change.

KATHERINE'S JOURNAL

It was after quitting time, and we were getting out of an all-day meeting where the Child Protective Services managers from around the state came to be told things. New policies, new guidelines, updates that everyone needed to know about – the usual stuff. It had been a long day and everyone was exhausted.

As I was gathering my stuff to go home, I noticed a crowd in the front of the room, and realized that one of our deputy directors was holding a tiny baby who was obviously only a couple days old. This tiny little girl had been born drug exposed and had to be brought to the hospital. She had been discharged and now needed to be transported to a foster home five hours away. The regional manager who worked in that county had been planning on spending the night in town, then making the long drive the next day. Instead, she was now going to drive the baby to the foster home – at night, by herself, after a full day of work.

I was dreading my own commute home, all one hour of it, sans newborn, and couldn't imagine my colleague's stamina. I asked her how she was going to do it. She looked exhausted, but just shrugged and gave a little smile. "I guess I'll just figure it out," she said.

I cried the whole hour drive home, because we live in a world that would require someone to drive a newborn baby for five hours at night, to a stranger's home. It is so comforting to know that there are people in the world like the manager who are willing to sacrifice their own comfort to take care of someone else's child.

The next day I was having lunch with one of my friends who works in the field. I told her how upset I was about the baby, and she just looked at me incredulously.

"You were traumatized by that? That kind of thing happens multiple times a day, every day," she said.

And I knew that. I'm the data person. I know how many infants come into care every year. But it is so different to see these children and these workers in person, instead of as numbers on a computer screen.

The woman who drove the newborn baby for five hours by herself at night didn't have a parade thrown for her. Social workers don't have people running up to them asking for autographs. But they do heroic things every day.

Child Welfare 2.0

One of the biggest threats to confront city dwellers in the last few hundred years didn't come from disease or poor sanitation or crime. It came from a terror that could strike at any time, spread quickly, and wipe out entire sections of major cities. There was precious little our ancestors could do to stop it, but today, it is such a small problem that we almost never worry about it.

Give up? It's fire.

Fire used to be incredibly common, and very hard to control. Single fires took out large sections of Detroit, Boston, and Chicago in the 1800s. The Great Chicago Fire alone destroyed over three square miles. A fire in Seattle in 1889 consumed the entire downtown. Gold Rush-era San Francisco also had a series of "Great Fires."

Naturally, people worked hard to address this obvious problem. Volunteer fire departments sprang up in the 1700s, with one of them founded by none other than Ben Franklin. Some rural areas still use that volunteer model, though larger towns and cities eventually professionalized their fire departments. Bit by bit, we got pretty good at putting out fires, and the equally important work of keeping them from spreading. It was a great step forward, to be sure. If you happen to visit a historical society museum and see an exhibit about a "Great Fire," odds are good it happened in the 1800s, then nevermore. Buildings still burned, but the neighbors didn't worry nearly as much.

Child welfare departments operate on a similar model. If there is something very bad happening to a kid right now, a simple phone call can bring a rush of professionals to the scene, and they will seek to contain the damage. The "fire" in this case is a different sort of devastating, but those professionals will try to put it out all the same. And while this system has its problems, we can all be proud that it exists. Having child trauma first responders is a very good thing indeed.

The catch here is that firefighters are only part of the reason we hardly worry about fire anymore. Over the last few hundred years, we have made a multi-pronged, parallel effort to prevent fires from starting in the first place. We dramatically changed how society did things – all kinds of things – often at great expense, and those efforts paid off handsomely.

Besides starting a volunteer fire department, Ben Franklin also pioneered the lightning rod, a metal conductor perched on the top of a building that delivered the amperage safely into the ground. Over time, we changed the way we built houses, mandating more fire-proof materials, smoke detectors, and sprinkler systems. The electrical code itself is not published by a government or a trade union, but by an outfit called the National Fire Protective Association, a collaboration started by a group of fire insurance companies in the late 1800s. Every few years, they ratchet up their standards with the publication of a new code book, recently including the mandate that all houses be constructed with arc-fault breakers, which shut off a circuit when arcing is detected, not just when too much juice is flowing. And in just the last 20 years, Congress and states have acted to make sure that cigarettes sold in the country basically put themselves out if left unattended. Even Smokey Bear's awareness efforts probably helped, though he, of course, focused on wildland fires.

It's hard to understate just how good we are at fire prevention these days. In 1975, long after Boston had professionalized its fire department, there were 417 reported fires. In 2013, the combination of codes and standards had brought that number down to 40.

Firefighters still respond to lots of emergency calls, but they usually have nothing to do with fires. Some fiscal hawks are even wondering if we couldn't get by with fewer firefighters.

When it comes to child welfare departments, this represents a critical step not taken, with tragic results. Most departments think of themselves as brigades of childhood trauma firefighters, responsible for intervention and treatment. Prevention, they say, is somebody else's problem. And they are not wrong: Plenty of politicians and other departments could and should be doing more about this. Furthermore, the vast majority of federal funding for child welfare is specifically for foster care reimbursement (though this is slowly changing). In many ways, child welfare departments are not funded for prevention.

But child welfare departments, who are for the most part staffed by some of the most dedicated and caring people on the planet, are in a unique position to lead this fight. They have the moral authority that comes from working with society's most troubled kids every day. More critically, they are sitting on stacks of data that can both help them do their jobs better and enlist politicians and members of the public in efforts to do more.

Fire departments know this. They could hide behind their mandates to do intervention and treatment, but they don't. Fire officials will happily talk, to anyone willing to listen, about fire prevention until they're blue in the face. They send out speakers to community groups. They send cute mascots (and not just Smokey) to county fairs and community festivals, hoping to get the next generation involved. And planners who work for the fire department keep an eye on new construction, even checking to make sure road widths are big enough to accommodate the trucks. They are thoroughly involved on the prevention side.

The Solution

But how could a child welfare department begin to act more like their holistic comrades at the fire department? Our modest proposal is this: An in-house unit of a few staffers (staff size would depend on the size of the entire agency workforce and contracted partnering agencies) that is dedicated to a process called continuous quality improvement (CQI). Their mandate would be to use data to identify problems and solutions. They would be engaged in the four-step process of assessing, planning, acting and evaluating progress toward measurable and meaningful results. Their jobs, quite simply, would be to help everyone else do their jobs better, and to enlist elected officials and the general public in that cause.

The CQI unit would bring together the persistent positivity of a life coach, the discipline of an inspector general, and the passion of an evangelist. It would have carte blanche to look at every piece of paper and bit of data the department produced. It would have some degree of political independence, so as to avoid meddling from the people whose feathers it would need to ruffle. And critically, it would have some control over the department's web site.

The tasks of this CQI unit could be broadly broken up into three key areas: assessment and evaluation, planning and action, and publicity/transparency. Let's tackle all three.

Assessment and Evaluation: The mission here is to emulate the work of the inspectors general that monitor big federal agencies by comparing the stated goals of the department with the reality on the ground. The critiques mentioned above, of course, are a good place to start. The CQI unit is perfectly positioned to hop on the internal computer network and calculate the investigator-to-case ratio. It can do a sampling of incoming call logs and determine whether they're going to the right place and if any are falling through the cracks. It can take a close look at the technology the department uses, and whether it causes minimal or unacceptable levels of friction where productivity is concerned. It can evaluate staff morale, a not insignificant factor in any organization, much less one dedicated to rushing toward human suffering. And it can conduct performance audits of the foster parent recruitment system, testing response times and soliciting feedback from parents on their user experience. It will take note of how many kids are repeatedly entering foster homes as opposed to less desirable group homes.

Those are the obvious areas to take a look at, but as an in-house unit, the CQI team will also be in a position to keep an ear to the ground, listening for communication breakdowns within the department, budgetary problems, and whatever else it picks up in its process of assessing, planning, acting, and evaluating.

Planning and Action: We don't envision this unit as a rock throwing, finger-pointing group. A key part of the mission would be training employees in the CQI process itself. As we've been saying over and over again in this book, every single job ever devised can be improved with deliberate application of the basic enlightenment principles embedded in CQI.

We've actually run programs to this effect in child welfare departments – they were designed to evaluate every corner of the agency. And while holding courses about the nebulous topic of "how you can do your jobs better" may seem like a disorganized way to get to the point, you'd be surprised at how quickly participants zero in on whatever their biggest challenge happens to be. We just teach them how to do all that zeroing in through planning and research of best practices, and how to use good information and good arguments to affect good changes. In fact, we call participants "Data Leaders."

For the CQI units, we envision a kind of ongoing Data Leaders Program with an emphasis on information analysis, research, and communication with colleagues, partners, and the public. All over the United States, and even the world, talented people are coming up with great new ideas for how to help kids and their families. Efforts to seek out those ideas and implement them are always a bit scattershot, but the CQI unit will institutionalize the never-ending struggle to get better, by alerting administrators to problems and training staffers directly to address them.

By the way, we see no reason why this research on best practices could not at the same time come up with strategies that other agencies could use to help the child welfare cause. It could not, of course, get involved in political campaigns to, for example, raise this or that tax to fund universal preschool. It could not advocate for the upping of payments to behavioral health providers who take Medicaid. But it could make sure that everyone knew exactly what those reforms would do for children if enacted.

Publicity and transparency: Assessment, Planning, Action and Evaluation are great things, to be sure, but they are primarily internal functions, and depend on cooperation from the old guard. But rest assured that the mission of the CQI unit does not depend entirely on asking nicely. With publicity, and the sort of partnerships with members of the media commonly cultivated by inspectors general at the federal level, the unit can really put some firepower into reforms, all while drawing productive attention to the department itself. Rather than staying out of the news, the CQI Unit would seek to publicize what's working and how partners and the public can collaborate to strengthen the lives of every child.

This is where some degree of control over the agency's web site comes into critical play. In the course of its normal day, the CQI unit will be harvesting a great deal of data, and they need to put that information (while protecting confidential personal data) on the web in a visually compelling way that's easy for non-professionals to understand. How many kids are in custody right now, broken down by zip code, county or region? What's the investigator caseload and workload? What's the average duration of a case? How many kids are at risk for aging out of the system without a permanent home? What's the breakdown between kids in foster care and kids in group homes? And what do the trends look like over the last year, or last five years, or in other states?

We need all these numbers in one place, with lots of colorful charts and graphs and plain-language explainers of technical terms. It should be updated every week, if not every day. It's all public information, after all, and with a little persistence you yourself could acquire it and put up the data on a web site you launch yourself. But given how hard that would be, and that we live in an era where newspapers increasingly don't have the staff to watch the government, it is the job of the government to show you what it's doing.

Think of this array of numbers as a dashboard readout – a quick check of vital signs. It's the equivalent of driving around town looking at potholes and verifying on-time performance of buses to assess transportation policy, except it's right there on the web. It won't tell you everything – after all, you can't check the fluids in the buses or make sure road crews are following best asphalt pouring practices – but it's a good temperature check that's always there and will never get buried on page A16 of one newspaper on one day and then be forgotten.

This sort of preemptive transparency is hardly a revolutionary thought, of course. Governments of all kinds routinely disclose campaign finance reports online without anybody asking for them. In New Mexico, the mayor of Albuquerque posted his monthly credit card statement on the city's web site. And there's also the National Debt Clock, a dramatic real-time illustration of our national debt and your particular share of it.

We need something like that for child welfare. A centralized clearinghouse with basic information is the sort of thing that attracts attention from journalists and politicians and members of the public looking for something to tweet. It turns an opaque and forgotten part of the government into something that everyone can see and touch. Agencies under that level of scrutiny tend to perform better. But if the administrators dislike that level of pressure, they may appreciate the flip side: Draconian budget cuts are harder to pull off when lawmakers and the general public actually know what you do all day and appreciate it. Those beloved firefighters learned that lesson a long time ago.

But this web site would be more than just a set of numbers paired with pretty charts and graphs. During the four-step process of CQI, the unit would produce lots of reports on the agency's challenges and what can be done about them. They would also produce quite a bit of original research on what's being done elsewhere and how that compares and contrasts to the local jurisdiction. All of that should also be posted on the web site as well. The reports may need to be dry and long, aimed primarily at administrators and lawmakers, but a quick executive summary for public and media consumption could be added easily. The more people who know what's going on under the hood, the better the engine will run.

Not easy. Just vital.

We don't pretend that implementing a CQI unit would be easy. While state government is not the military, it is built on a chain-of-command model. If you have a problem or an innovative idea, you're supposed to go to your direct supervisor for guidance, not skip over a level of management, and you're certainly not supposed to put random internal information on the internet, even if it's public. Such organizations are resistant to change, and that's before we run into all the individuals who are just riding it out for a couple of years till retirement, or don't want to put in the extra work reform would require, or who just woke up on the wrong side of the bed one day twenty years ago and decided to make it a habit.

But if an idea like a fully-staffed and tech-empowered CQI unit can get through a legislature, it may well crack the code that the fire safety people figured out a long time ago. The folks behind that movement fought fires aggressively, but they also tried to prevent fires on many different fronts, including installing a fire safety research organization into the permanent regulatory structure. In other words, they planted a CQI unit into the equation, let it do its thing, and the fact that you probably worry much less about fire than your great grandparents did speaks for itself.

That's what we want for child welfare. We doubt that we'll live long enough to see trauma levels take a dive similar to fire rates, but we could set the table for it. We just need to make sure that continuous quality improvement is a permanent part of the process. We want to end the common practice of government agencies acting before assessing and planning. We want to end the practice of governments and foundations funding projects without a rigorous evaluation process. When child welfare is properly funded, correctly staffed to meet best practice guidelines, expertly infused with state-of-the-art technology, and allowed to use data to inform all actions, we will at long last have a vital agency of authority in a place to take the lead in preventing all forms of adverse childhood experiences and trauma.

There's a good chance investigator Susan will again wake up in the wee hours of the morning tomorrow and be rushed to another catastrophe, the repercussions of which could hurt society for decades hence. But we have it in our power to reduce the odds that she'll ever have to make such a trek, and we can also choose to make sure she has the tools both to help the kids find a safe place to stay, and to direct mom to the help she clearly needs. We can either make sure she works in an agency where data informs action and empowerment is pervasive, or we can wait for the next call to the motel, hoping against hope that this time it does not go terribly, fatally wrong.

KATHERINE'S JOURNAL
After my time overseeing data and research in a child welfare department, I was shocked by how many people who work in the foundation and nonprofit world had no idea how pervasive child abuse is. A peer reviewed study found that maltreatment will be confirmed for one in eight children in the United States. That's an average of 3 children in each classroom, in each school, in each city. And even people who are experts at teaching kids, at feeding kids, and helping kids with medical issues have no idea that this is so pervasive. Kids can't learn if they are hungry. They also can't learn if they are afraid. If we want to improve outcomes for kids – graduation rates, teen pregnancy rates, drug use, or anything else, we must first make sure that they are safe, and that they feel safe.

Chapter Six

_____

Trauma's fuel tank:
The ongoing crisis in
mental health care

Anna's Story

Anna's mother, Cassandra, had a very long history of mental health problems. Passing year after year through elementary, middle, and high school, she might have appeared to her teachers like another disinterested student from a tough neighborhood, but she was a troubled, tormented soul. We don't know what interventions, if any, took place in school to address her emotional state, but we do know that by the time she entered the juvenile justice system, she was also entering a dramatic downward spiral. There was never an extensive review (at least not one ever made public) of all of Cassandra's adverse childhood experiences, but we can surmise she too was a victim of trauma to some degree. We do know she had many drug related arrests, made several calls to police about domestic violence, and spent some time in jail. What we don't know about Cassandra and what we still don't know about today's children is just how many live in households where access to behavioral health care could make a huge difference in preventing trauma.

NATHAN IS 11, and a rather average boy. He watches a lot of TV, doesn't do much in the way of extracurricular activities, and doesn't read for pleasure. When describing him, his teachers do not reach for his various spectacular feats of academia, since there are none. But they do not groan or roll their eyes either, as there are no major discipline issues. They generally settle for the default option for the unremarkable and refer to him as a "good kid."

For Nathan's first ten years, he lived with his mother in a small apartment in a part of town full of strip malls dotted with pharmacies, Chinese restaurants and personal injury lawyers. Mom was generally able to hold down jobs, but they tended not to last for more than eight months or so, and they never paid well. Nathan's father, meanwhile, has never really been in the picture, and they don't talk about him much.

Nathan is in excellent physical health, which is partly thanks to genetics, and partly thanks to pretty good health insurance, having been on Medicaid for his entire life. Medicaid, the federal/state insurance partnership for low-income people, saw to it that he was born in a modern first-world hospital, and paid for all his vaccinations and regular checkups. It also paid to treat a fairly normal collection of childhood illnesses, including a couple of ear infections and a skinned knee that required some stitches.

And for this we can most certainly be proud. Nathan is growing up in poverty in a tough situation, but we as a society, going back to the days of Lyndon Johnson, have seen fit to make sure that Nathan doesn't need to add "easily preventable medical problems" to his list of things to worry about. We did not make him and his mother beg on the streets for help curing an ear infection or stitching up a leg. Maybe we were motivated by pangs of guilt, or maybe we just didn't want to physically see them on the street, but one way or another, we figured it would just be better to pay for it and move on. It was a moral and practical victory.

But Nathan is by no means out of the woods yet. His mother basically kept it together until he was about seven, but then descended into a drug habit that sucked up her time and money and became a serious case of neglect by the time Nathan turned ten. For several years, there was often no food in the house, and Nathan had to take charge of getting himself to school. Mom was not so great about getting him to doctor's appointments either, though luckily there weren't many to worry about. Nathan ended up spending a lot of time at the home of his aunt, who conveniently lived just under a mile away.

Things eventually came to a head with mom's drug habit. Child protective services got involved, and now Nathan lives with that aunt instead of just visiting all the time. And while he gets enough to eat and has the help he needs getting to school and to medical appointments, he will very soon need much more than that.

Challenges we face

More than ever in this modern world, our success in life depends on getting along with other people, and that makes a clean bill of mental health all the more important. When mental health challenges go untreated or misdiagnosed, it's a recipe for thin social networks, reduced opportunities, and troubled romantic relationships. Depression and addiction may not be far behind. Nathan may face a daunting mental health future, and it's easy to see how it could turn out badly for him, for society at large, and his future kids.

Already, Nathan has stacked up a pile of ACEs. He (1) witnessed the messy separation of his parents, (2) watched his father go to prison, (3) lived with someone who abused substances, and (4) suffered neglect when food ran out. It gets worse for some American kids, but this is well within the danger zone.

The good news, however, is that Nathan is still just 11, and finally lives in a stable environment. The other bit of good news is that we know what Nathan needs: A stable reliable home, an adult who cares about him, and a therapist. Maybe this therapist will need prescription-writing authority, or maybe not. Whomever they are, they will know where Nathan is coming from, and will help guide him through the mental minefield that life has placed him in. And this will take time.

If he can find a qualified mental health care professional, stick with treatment, do his part of the work in therapy, and find a strong circle of social support, he has a good chance of addressing the trauma and establishing a healthy coping mechanism for himself. Mental health care does not work with the efficiency of the shingles vaccine, but still, the results can be impressive if the match of client and counselor is right. Right now, Nathan may actually blame himself for this trauma. If a therapist can just help him come to terms with the reality of his non-responsibility for his mother's actions, it will represent great progress that can help him have a better life.

Humans have always boasted a capacity to talk ourselves into adapting to new realities. Once upon a time many years ago, we all thought using a toilet was impossibly intimidating. As teens, the prospect of romantic relationships may have terrified us. So did trying to find work or going off to college, or, presumably, walking over the land bridge to North America. But through a long, gentle series of nudges in the right direction, we got there, and we got used to it. Using the same human brain software and taking incremental steps, there's a good chance Nathan can get better at forming and maintaining the sort of relationships that will help him find better jobs, achieve good grades, get a job, pay taxes, fight with his romantic partners less, and raise healthier kids. All we have to do is get him in a room with professionals who know, quite literally, what they're talking about. Warren Buffett never saw an investment opportunity this good.

But despite our enviable first world institutions and growing awareness of mental health as a real thing, we as a country are still fantastically bad at making that access happen, thanks to a combination of built-in challenges, our own incompetence, and an unproductive (though understandable) belief that people should just solve their own problems.

Let's start at the beginning: If Nathan is going to ever get to that therapist's office, somebody is going to have to notice the problem. With the skinned knee that required stitches, Nathan noticed the problem right away and was only too happy to bring it to the attention of others. But he is much less likely to recognize the aftereffects of neglect. The other person in a good position to do something – his mother – was busy pursuing a drug habit. His aunt/guardian might help, but she might also dismiss Nathan's behavior as "the way he is." It may also be that he acts more normally around a trusted family member than others – these things can be pretty subtle sometimes. That leaves us with a teacher who is also busy keeping track of 29 other kids, or perhaps a marching band instructor or youth pastor who might be in the same situation. (This is actually the most likely scenario, especially if the teachers in question have been trained to spot ACEs or maltreatment. That sort of training is lacking more often than not, and the quality can be spotty even when it's there). Maybe an extended family member will say something, or maybe they don't even live in the same town. In any event, telling a guardian something like "I think Nathan has a mental health problem" is a lot more challenging than "don't forget that Nathan will need his tetanus booster soon." So the most obvious result comes to pass, and kids fall through the cracks without the help they need.

Even if this problem is successfully flagged, there is another layer to the logistics onion. Many medical appointments are one-and-done affairs, especially for kids, who have an enviable ability to bounce back from all kinds of scary-looking illnesses in record time. They go, they get diagnosed, some cure that our great grandparents could only dream of is administered, and they get better. Behavioral health, on the other hand, requires schlepping back to that office every week, or every month, for a long time, which is precisely the sort of task that people like Nathan's mom are worst at, even if they can be persuaded to take the whole business seriously.

There is also a very serious matter of money. In one sense, behavioral health is cheap, because it's just one person in an ordinary room conveniently devoid of $1 million MRI machines and platoons of nurses or assistants (though setting up a behavioral health practice, especially in psychiatry, is no easy or inexpensive task). Sometimes pharmacies get involved, but that's usually just the psychiatrists. Overhead is so low that some behavioral health providers even do their own billing. Nobody need toil away at protracted fights over billing codes like they do in hospitals. In an era when the average emergency room visit costs about $1,200, a professional counselor in a nondescript room seems like a bargain.

But on the other hand, the necessity of frequent appointments means that behavioral health can be very expensive for patients. Every visit could require some sort of payment. If your insurance is Medicaid, the payment may be zero or perhaps some token few dollars. If you make too much money for Medicaid, there may be only a copayment – perhaps $50. But that is probably a lot of money for Nathan's aunt, even if she makes more than a Medicaid level income.

The almost-worst case scenario is a catastrophic insurance policy that makes you pay full price for all appointments until you hit a deductible, usually a few thousand dollars.

The absolute worst case scenario is no insurance at all. Thanks to the expansion of the Children's Health Insurance Program, a close cousin of Medicaid, this is less of a problem for kids (roughly 5 percent uninsured) than adults (roughly 10 percent). But most of those 5 percent live in families that have a very difficult time navigating life and are often very poor. They may qualify for Medicaid but lack the wherewithal to fill out the forms. Sometimes there is another factor in play, like being an undocumented immigrant. In any event, they're likely to need help the most, but given that a year's worth of weekly appointments may cost in the neighborhood of $5,000, it's probably a bridge too far.

What this all means to Nathan and his aunt (who, remember, wants to help) is that doing the right thing is the hardest option that can possibly be taken. Most likely, nothing will happen, and Nathan can't afford that. Perhaps more to the point, we taxpayers can't afford not to help.

Let's for just a minute imagine that what Nathan needs to stay off hard drugs and graduate from high school (an admittedly low bar) is a monthly appointment until he's 18. Let's also say that we can get his mother for some of those appointments, and half as many on her own, since she's part of the equation and working with parents is a proven way to improve outcomes. Over eight years, that's 144 appointments, at an estimated cost of $75 per session. That's $10,800 spent by society.

If Nathan overdoses on a hard drug and requires hospitalization even one time, we'll spend much more than that. A year in jail, meanwhile, will cost about $22,000. But if Nathan graduates from high school, he'll make on average $7,000 more per year, meaning his extra Social Security taxes alone will pay that money back in 20 years, leaving another 25 years for society to actually make money on that mental health investment. By the time he retires, we'll be looking at about a 120 percent return on our money. Like we said, Warren Buffet never saw an opportunity this good.

Hurdle after Hurdle

So to review: For behavioral health care to be effective, uninsured kids are most likely going to need the same parents who can't get it together to keep food in the fridge to somehow plow through a mountain of complicated enrollment paperwork. Nobody's holding their breath on that one. And Nathan has that extra complicated family situation to deal with as well.

Even those with comprehensive insurance and a willingness to make mental health care happen may run into a shortage of providers or other similarly stark barriers. They may call around and not find a provider that is taking new patients. They may find a provider who is taking new patients but not taking Medicaid. They may get put on a waiting list, or given an appointment months from now. The provider may be inconveniently located, leading to transportation difficulties. Residents of rural areas might be in even worse shape, jealous of the city folk who merely have to drive across town, instead of to the next town. Especially in less populated western states, the nearest provider might be hours away.

If all those hurdles can be vanquished, there is still the enduring stigma of mental illness that we can't seem to quite shake off society's back. There's progress, to be sure, but it's maddeningly slow. And it's hard to get excited over healthcare that doesn't really involve cures. We like cures and find them endlessly attractive. But it's hard to get motivated by a long and tedious talk therapy process that often (to paraphrase Freud) just transforms misery into common unhappiness, and considers this a great success. (We know, for the record, that behavioral healthcare is much more than this. In its many forms, these therapies can be not only transformative and healing, but give people a second chance at a productive and happy life.)

In sum, we see two main problems here. One is a money problem, which can probably only be comprehensively solved at the federal or state level. Another is a logistics problem, which is the sort of thing that can be solved at a local level without an act of Congress, then hopefully replicated all over the place. More on money later, but first, logistics.

Back to school

Let's make this easy: We believe that America can take a big and fairly simple bite out of this problem by installing behavioral health services in schools, and streamlining the process by which kids and their family members get access to services.

Schools already have counselors, but they tend to focus on testing, academic planning, college applications, and the like. Some schools have a resident social worker who may be covering numerous schools. And just like the social workers we met in the previous chapter, their caseloads are often much too high to allow for effective psychological work. Coverage is spotty, and it's not what we're talking about anyway.

We would instead like to see regular psychologists, psychiatrists, and other counselors actually set up practices for kids and their families right in the schools. Once the final bell rings, there is usually plenty of space to be had, but every school we've ever been to could probably fit a few providers in during the day as well. (We know of one school that did counseling in a surprisingly ample former janitorial supply closet.) Under this scenario, the school would not need to hire the practitioners, but rather just give them space and let them bill insurance just like they always do. (For the uninsured or those with catastrophic policies, it would be helpful to establish a subsidized, sliding scale fee structure, but this is of course a separate and bigger logistical issue involving more money.)

This sort of school-based operation would go a long way toward removing the practical and psychological barriers to behavioral healthcare. Finding a provider can be a pain, but much less so if you already know where one or two of them practice. Transportation to a provider's office can be hard as well, both because it could be far away and because it could require extra emotional energy learning a new place and how to get there. But that's not the case if they work at the school.

This system would also reduce the logistical burden of parents, who often don't have the resources to make the health care happen in the first place. Their role would be reduced from critical to optional. Today, if a teacher or school nurse recommends to a parent that a child get some help, it is usually up to the parent to make the phone calls and arrange for transportation. If the provider worked at a school, it could be as simple as sending the parent a courtesy heads up that the health care was happening. (This would work primarily for Medicaid in circumstances that did not involve copayments. We are definitely not proposing that schools conspire to rack up large bills behind parent's backs.)

For extra credit, something we know education professionals love, there are a few other things they could do to ensure that all students found the care they needed in order to succeed in school.

- Collect health insurance information during school registration and get permission to forward it to the on-site providers. That will save a step later.
- Arrange for an insurance enroller (who can do both Medicaid and Affordable Care Act exchange coverage) to visit from time to time and make sure those families without insurance get it.
- Arrange for rides home for the kids who stay after school for appointments. (It might just be the same bus that the football team uses to get home.)
- Think about throwing the doors open to primary care health care providers as well.
- If you have kids who need help and are unable to get insured, see if the district or some other entity (like a local foundation, hospital community outreach department, or non-profit working in youth development) will supplement care.

There are lots of models for school-based health care out there, and if we had a magic wand, we would actually do something more comprehensive than this. But we still like the model because it has a very low barrier to entry. Schools can just let practitioners use space they weren't using anyway, and maybe do a little logistical work on the side. No funding streams to manage unless someone really wants to go above and beyond the call of duty. But for the "ideal world" version of this, if you want to learn more, we recommend a quick search on "full-service community schools" and "school-based health centers."

DOM'S JOURNAL
I have long since ceased to be surprised by some state's lack of commitment to mental health care for our most vulnerable parents. While there are states and cities building the capacity to address untreated mental health challenges, others are sorely trailing behind. Agencies might do a full mental health assessment on parents whose children were taken into custody, which sounds prudent, except that is also exactly where it ends in some jurisdictions. If problems are found during the assessment (which is common), those highly vulnerable and dysfunctional people are told to find somewhere to get help, get themselves there, and figure out how to pay for it. Even with a kind social worker helping with navigation, those are some pretty wide cracks, and people are all but guaranteed to fall through, especially in low income and rural areas.

While this chapter is focused on mental health care, helping families cope with ACEs may also involve making sure that lower income parents are linked up with safe shelter, a stable food supply, affordable transportation options, and help finding and keeping a job. What this means is that each community needs to not only build up its mental health network to address ACEs, but also make sure that families as a whole get the help they need, which will also help to address ACEs. We're not saying that schools need to become full-fledged social service agencies (without bigger budgets and staffs at least). But each district needs to know that at least half of their student population has or soon will endure ACEs, and that help is required.

Supply and demand

This idea of putting behavioral health services in schools (which, admittedly, is not original to us) is great, and we're obviously big fans, but it will get absolutely nowhere unless we address a broader problem: There aren't enough providers out there. There are about 3,000 counties in the United States, and a significant number of them have little to no behavioral health practitioners at all.

The shortage has two components. First, there are simply not enough mental health care providers overall to meet demand. That will be doubly true (or more) over time, because we are an optimistic bunch and think that awareness of good mental health treatments will continue to grow and actually translate into more patients looking for help. The more people like Prince Harry travel around giving interviews about mental health (one of his projects) the more we like our chances.

Private insurance, Medicare, and Medicaid: What's working and what's not

How to increase the supply of providers? As mentioned above, that's a money problem, and specifically, a Medicaid money problem. While most kids are covered by private plans through employers or the exchanges, about 40 percent of those under age 18 are on Medicaid. (The program also pays for half of all births.) Forty percent may sound like a lot, but it's even bigger than you think. Because of the inextricable connection between poverty and mental health, Medicaid actually turns out to be the single largest buyer of mental health services in the country. The trouble is, they don't pay much for it.

Insurance reimbursement rates are incredibly complicated, and they vary by state, but here's the drive-by version: For any given service, private insurance usually pays the most. For this reason, doctors and hospitals love private insurance, but needless to say those companies don't pay that much because they love doctors. They pay because they have so little leverage in the marketplace that they can be efficiently squeezed for all they're worth.

Next on the list comes Medicare, which pays less and only covers people under 65 if they're disabled. Providers say disparaging things about Medicare, and they accept it a little less often than private insurance, but participation rates are still very high. Providers often still advertise for new Medicare patients, leading us to believe that all the bellyaching has to do with the fact that Medicare can't be pushed around like the private insurers.

Finally on that list comes Medicaid, which pays significantly less than Medicare. Providers still complain about not being able to make a living on Medicaid rates, but it rings truer than when they talk about Medicare. Of course, it's not technically true: Plenty of providers see tons of Medicaid patients while managing to pay the office light bill and put gas in the tank. They make a living, but the overall shortage strongly suggests that it's not a particularly great living relative to the other career options they have at their disposal.

So how do we fix this? Here are some promising ideas:

Idea One: Raise reimbursement rates. It's an obvious solution, but we should mention it anyway. Pay providers more to do mental health care, and soon there will magically be more of them. The advantage of this cure is its simplicity, except for the part about it probably involving an act of Congress and a great deal of money. One less expensive alternative would be to just raise rates for providers in rural areas, where shortages are particularly acute.

Idea Two: Other incentives for future providers. Medical education is expensive, and we could offer substantial help in exchange for, say, five to ten years of service after graduation devoted to practicing in a rural or otherwise underserved area. There are already models out there ripe for the searching. One of them may work for your region.

That's it for the obvious stuff. From here, we get creative. Maybe even crazy.

Idea Three: Telemedicine: This could, in theory, play an important role in getting services to rural areas. Most of what you need for behavioral health can be done over Skype, and your counselor could be in Phoenix or Pittsburgh (or Bangalore or Cape Town for that matter). Programs that actually implement that idea seem to be scattered and very new, and there are surely problems that will need ironing out, but it could be part of a solution that distributes behavioral health out from the urban areas.

Idea Four: Broadening the definition of caregiver. Talk therapy is not the exclusive domain of people with various letters after their names. Priests and other faith leaders have been doing it since the days when "medicine" was basically just a few people carrying around bags of herbs and leeches. Most of us have friends or family members that are particularly good at helping us talk things through. Twelve step groups are also a kind of talk therapy. Some colleges train "peer counselors" to administer less formal help to other students. If we can get these people deployed and talking to others, it may free up capacity.

Idea Five: Artificial intelligence. Chatbot "coaches" have been used to help Syrian refugees and some college students, so why not other groups? There would be some safeguards to put in place, to be sure, but if it works, it works.

DOM'S JOURNAL
One of my client organizations had recently won some funding to do mental health referral training – a technique called "Mental Health First Aid." They were eager to do trainings all over the state, help people, and no doubt do all kinds of other intuitively great things. The training program

itself was great. It efficiently helped school staff identify signs of mental stress, depression, and suicidal feelings.

But it came with an optimistic warning: Do not deploy unless you have enough mental health providers in the area to handle the bump in demand. I shared those concerns, fearing that the training really was that good. "We most certainly would not be advocating for residents to take an HIV test if these tests were not available, right?" I said. I suggested doing assessments of mental health capacity in the various target communities before doing all the outreach.

The client went ahead with the training anyway, despite knowing of mental health care provider scarcity. After all, the federal funding was for training, not provider capacity. As a result, nothing much happened. People learned about mental health, then learned there wasn't much they could do about it.

Mental health is a crucial part of the overall ACEs picture. We are an adaptable bunch, and many of us can literally talk ourselves into healthier habits where we would otherwise harm ourselves and others. That means better relationships, better economic prospects, more taxes paid, and fewer crimes committed. We just need to connect three dots together: Kids, parents, and providers. Those connections are tenuous and shaky right now, but with a push from schools and a little creativity in the greater community, we could strengthen them immeasurably, even without help from Congress.

We should get busy, in other words, and we should get busy now. Awareness of mental health is still too low, and most of our states lack the sort of intelligent, well-funded group that can educate the public and politicians about these matters.

KATHERINE'S JOURNAL
The United Nations isn't usually associated with mental health awareness, but they actually have some recommendations on the matter: Build community mental health services, they say. Develop them in general hospitals. Integrate mental health services into primary care centers. Build informal community mental health services and promote self-care with technology, especially the kind that

can be used on mobile phones. The recommendations were aimed at developing countries, of course, but here's the kicker: We should follow them, too. All of them.

Work on the stigma

We know that in some communities the idea of telling family secrets to a stranger (like a mental health care provider) is just not acceptable. Domestic violence, abuse, neglect, substance misuse among house-hold members – this is not the business of outsiders. People fear that speaking up will lead to a call to child protective services or other law enforcement – even immigration authorities. Others fear losing control over their spouses and children. We have not done a good job explaining how mental health care works, and so we have some very targeted and long term public education to do – especially in communities hardest hit by ACEs.

Stigmas, meanwhile, are all-too-often reinforced by TV dramas that imply mental illness is synonymous with mayhem and murder. (The reality, of course, is that mental illness is much more likely to look like someone who is unspeakably sad or paralyzed with anxiety, all of which would, of course, make for very bad television.)

But this is changing, with every prominent public figure that talks about his or her own struggle, and every new primary care provider who screens new patients for it. Meanwhile, our hyper-connected world is more and more capable of absorbing dramatic change very quickly. The right celebrity story or hashtag could well set off a quantum leap in mental health awareness, and we hope it does. It took Magic Johnson opening up about AIDS, after all, to shock the world into finally coming to terms with the epidemic, many years after gay men and their friends were advocating for compassionate care for those with AIDS.

Consequences

This tipping point cannot come soon enough. Even if you're blessed with excellent mental health, you're paying the price as well. We lose about $190 billion in economic productivity every year because we're not connecting the dots that connect back to untreated trauma and mental health challenges. That's before we shell out for the emergency rooms, the hospitals, the child welfare agencies, the cops, the prosecutors, the judges, and the prisons.

And there is a final cost, born by us all, of looking an 11-year-boy in the face and telling him we can't help. When we do that, we dishonor his potential and lie to ourselves. In a nation as wealthy, creative and technologically advanced as ours, we have no legitimate excuse for not ensuring the mental health care of every child and adult.

Chapter Seven

_____

Because this is America: Why your zip code should not determine your destiny

Anna's Story

When she was not in foster care or with her mother, Anna often found herself in the care of her mother's relatives. For years, it seems, there were many adults in her life, and while some of them were worried, none were able to prevent her mother from murdering her. We can only imagine how things might have been different if her mother had access to a home visitation program when Anna was born. Perhaps this trained caregiver could have helped connect Cassandra with services to help her deal with her postpartum depression. And if Anna had been in a quality early childhood education program, perhaps those educators might have stepped in to intervene when signs of problems became apparent. Or, if Anna had a long-term mentor from an agency like Big Brothers Big Sisters in her life – visiting her weekly over a number of years – this "big sister," from outside the dysfunctional extended family, might have been able to intervene in time. There are a lot of "ifs" in this scenario, but we know this much: When a second, third, or fourth pair of well-trained eyes are on a child, those kids have a better shot at avoiding Anna's fate.

WE HUMANS get all sorts of satisfaction basking in the glow of our accomplishments. Major breakthroughs at work, minor home improvements, or a college paper deep in the memory banks – we all enjoy replaying how we metaphorically (or sometimes literally) knocked it out of the park. But those of us with college days to look back on, homes to improve, and great jobs to have breakthroughs at tend to overlook our greatest accomplishment of all: Being born in the right zip code. (And that's just pure luck!)

That work presentation may have wowed the crowd, but your decision (which of course wasn't your decision at all) to be born in the right place to the right parents merits the sort of standing ovation normally reserved for gold medal winners at the Olympics. Seriously, that was a super critical decision that changed darn near everything in your life for the better, and you crushed it. You could have chosen 87121, like some total bonehead, but instead you probably chose parents (emphasis on the plural) who took you home to a place like 87048.

There's a lot to love about 87048. Let's do a quick comparison:

	87048	87121	USA
Percent with high school diploma or better	94.3%	73.3%	86.7%
Median household income	$79,792	$40,816	$53,889
Poverty rate	7.1%	25.4%	15.5%

These two zip codes are actually a short drive from each other. One is the southwest corner of Albuquerque, and the other is a well-heeled bedroom community on the north side of the metro area. But you didn't need to know that to know that only one has great schools, beautiful infrastructure, and houses that are reasonably up to code. Only one has streets that you probably wouldn't mind walking after dark.

While childhood trauma occurs across all socio-economic levels, high ACEs scores are often associated with poverty, and you're more likely to find that in 87121. (But you will find trauma in 87048.) The difference is another story you've heard before: The systems for cushioning the blow – both in formal governmental and nonprofit programs, and families and friends informally looking out for each other – are probably much better in that tight bedroom community.

Resourced parents just raise their kids differently. (And here we should emphasize that "resourced" in this chapter means a household containing two parents who probably went to college, and doesn't really have much to do with the numbers on a tax return.) They treat childrearing as a complex project requiring constant introspection, consultation with other parents, and researching of best practices. They occasionally carry this to positively annoying levels, as any childless person at a party full of parents can attest, but it's important work nonetheless.

Critically, resourced parents also seek to build a large universe of positive influences and mentors for their kids – a world-within-a-world that serves to educate, model good behavior, and occasionally step into surrogate parental roles. Children in this world will go to preschool, play after-school sports, and be shuttled around to a staggering list of other extra-curricular activities, including play dates with other kids who grow up in similar worlds. They will probably know at least a few adults who are not their parents yet are deeply invested in their success and can serve as confidants or connections to educational and work opportunities, both in youth and throughout life. Resourced parents will also see to it that their local governments do their part as well. The proverb that "it takes a village to raise a child" may be overused, but well-resourced parents know it's true. (This is not to say that parents without resources don't want what's best for their kids – just that it's so much harder for them to do the job.)

Deirdre

That sort of childhood sounds idyllic, and hopefully to your ears, totally normal. But consider what it looked like for Deirdre, the sort of person who is most likely found in the zip code you ingeniously chose not to grow up in. She is 21, and has been working as a clerk in a gas station for a few years since graduating from an underperforming high school. She was raised by a mother who struggled with untreated depression and addiction to painkillers. When her father was around, which was rare, he beat her. Suffice it to say that Deirdre's ACE score is off the charts, and all things considered, it's actually somewhat miraculous that she graduated and is gainfully (if humbly) employed.

But what of Deirdre's future? She has few friends and all kinds of trouble relating to others, since she never saw healthy behavior growing up. She had few professional connections, and her limited vocabulary and unfamiliarity with the customs of collaborative workplaces would have shut her out of those opportunities anyway. Some of her peers were lucky enough to be raised not just by parents, but by a parade of caring coaches, religious leaders, and family members, but Deirdre has no such network to turn to.

There is a much ballyhooed and yet mostly hypothetical scenario in which Deirdre turns this around with sheer force of personality. In this pleasant little daydream, she struggles through community college and into some reasonably well-paying trade, overcoming her considerable challenges to achieve the swelling greatness you've seen at the end of many movies. Such a bootstrap scenario has happened before, but it's rare, because few people have that sort of personality, and because we are all suggestable social creatures and generally do what those around us are doing. Typically in resourced families, the painstaking pursuit of higher education is instilled as an expectation from an early age, which is a nice way of saying we get pushed and borderline bullied into going to college and making something of ourselves. And given the immense and non-intuitive long-term challenge that higher education is, that semi-authoritarian nudging is probably a very necessary thing.

Deirdre, however, was left to her own devices, and took the most obvious career path, which is why she's at the gas station, looking down the road to a long career featuring similar jobs. Her wages through life will probably be low enough to qualify her for the Earned Income Tax Credit, food stamps, Medicaid, and other help. Even if she decisively escaped her childhood without an addiction or major mental health problem, she is still in big economic trouble for the long term. She grew up low income, with a series of bad inputs. Spinning her wheels in dead-end jobs is, tragically enough, something of a best case scenario.

There's one more wrinkle in the story of Deirdre at age 21: She is about to have a baby boy named Ethan, with a father already out of the picture. And this, dear reader, represents an inflection point for Deirdre and our society at large, so we all have some decisions to make.

One option would be to, as some surely would, rake Deirdre over the coals as an hopeless case. Some might say she is irresponsible, unqualified, and should have known better than to have a child before building up a life that's a little more stable than a rented efficiency in a under-resourced neighborhood and a job at a gas station. We can already hear some crusty cynic saying, "I'm sick of people who are not ready for parenting primetime having kids, and equally tired of subsidizing their mistakes."

Another option is to kick our empathy engines into overdrive and consider what a rough life Deirdre has had, remembering that there but for the grace of God go you. What would your life have been like without a father figure, save for the stranger who visited once in a blue moon and left you with bruises? What if your mother cared more about getting high than feeding you regularly? Would you really have bootstrapped your way to greatness from that hell?

We have a suggestion for which option to take: We don't care. This is less about Deirdre, and whether she's a mere burden on the system or a sympathetic lost soul, and more about soon-to-be-born Ethan. Neither anger nor empathy will give him the childhood we want him to have, so our suggestion is this: Feel whatever you want about Deirdre, then work like hell to build a country in which all zip codes are a great, or at least tolerable, place to grow up, so that 20 years from now, Ethan isn't in this exact same place as his mom.

How to do that? We've got three relatively simple suggestions. Then it gets complicated. Read on.

Idea One: Kids actually do come with instruction manuals

There is some truth in the old saw that kids don't come with instruction manuals, but not as much as you might think. Every child has their own inexplicable peculiarities, to be sure, and parents never tire of raving about them, but they're similar enough that a kind of manual of best practices does exist. It floats around conversation mills at backyard barbecues and new parent groups at churches. It is endlessly turned over on internet message boards. It spews forth from a vast industrial complex of baby and child advice books. And it is more formally maintained by our nation's impressive strategic reserves of pediatricians and the dedicated souls who staff nurse helplines.

Ethan needs Deirdre to get a piece of this action, and the best strategy we have for making that happen is something called home visitation. Essentially, that means sending a nurse or other well-trained professional or paraprofessional over to their home for a visit once a week for the first few years to ask questions, listen, and review parenting best practices. The home visitor is trying to make sure that Ethan is healthy, getting all his shots, and behaving more-or-less normally. (Ideally, this dovetails with prenatal care that Deirdre already hopefully received.)

At the same time, the home visitor is trying to make sure Deirdre is doing the little things that make all the difference. Babies need holding, feeding, and naps. They need to be read stories and talked to. They need to be kept away from unprotected electrical outlets and small things that they will inevitably put in their mouths and possibly choke on. They need to be kept far away from an intoxicated boyfriend who offers to babysit. When they cry or spit up or get a rash, there are procedures to follow, thanks to the great informal instruction manual. Two-year-olds have their own best practices, and there's another set for five-year-olds. Parents, especially single parents, need help too. They need a break every now and then, to take a shower by themselves, catch some sleep, and leave the house without the kids. Home visitors keep an eye on parents as well, making sure they catch those occasional breaks. They can also make sure Deirdre knows the best options for family planning so that little Ethan only has a sibling if she's ready for that.

It's quite possible that you're already well versed in these best practices. You're just sitting there, nodding your head, thinking "Well yea, electrical outlets need to be covered up. And the sky is blue." But here is an interesting question: How do you know this stuff? You may have seen this sort of behavior modeled your whole life with younger siblings, or you may have watched friends and asked lots of questions. You may have just called mom and dad all the time when you had kids and picked their brains. You may have even learned everything you needed to know on the internet. But think about this: all of those options are effectively cut off from some people. Many don't have the friends or the connections or are just not very good at researching stuff. The home visitor's job is to make sure Deirdre has some kind of onramp into that world and is keeping up.

It all seems so small and inconsequential – just one expert relating, modeling, and nudging a neophyte in the right direction. But we promise these little things move mountains. These chats can make the difference between Ethan growing up to work at a gas station and Ethan growing up to work at a bank. They make the difference between having a baby at 18 and having a baby at 28. They make the difference between low and medium or even high income, and thus the difference between being on public assistance for an entire lifetime or just a partial lifetime. As an added bonus, home visiting programs have been shown to directly decrease child abuse and neglect.

Happily, these visitation programs exist, but they are far from universal. Medicaid runs a pilot program in some parts of the country, as do some nonprofits. Meanwhile, there are about four million births every year in the United States, and nearly every set of parents could probably get some value out of a home visitation program. A large fraction of people with their own history of ACEs could get immense value out of such a program, and would return that value to the rest of society in spades. But this patchwork, as you might expect, leaves a large fraction uncovered.

We are using vague terms like "large fraction" because we're not aware of any comprehensive national assessment of how many kids and single parents out there desperately need such a visitation program. That said, it probably wouldn't be too hard to figure out at a small scale, so we encourage you to find an envelope and start scribbling on the back of it. If we take birth data by zip code or some other region and mix it up with poverty rates and the number of kids in protective custody, then cross reference it with the number of visitation slots available in a given area, we'd probably have a decent enough picture of the situation that could be replicable elsewhere. We'll talk later about how you might do this and other basic assessments in your community, but in general, we think this would be a great thing for the continuous quality improvement (CQI) unit we advocated for in the child welfare chapter to produce and publicize.

Knowing the numbers would be a good start, but no matter what they are, we still have a challenge in making sure that every new parent gets a visit. One option is for individual cities or states to raise some money and just hire the administrators, nurses, and other experts, and make it happen that way, and we like that idea. Still, we like this simpler solution even more: make it a standardized health benefit on insurance plans, and make sure it doesn't cost extra to use.

Congress did something along these lines a few years back when it passed the Affordable Care Act, more commonly known as Obamacare. With that law, it standardized the definition of health insurance to a specific list of ten "essential health benefits." In other words, if a health insurance company wanted to sell something and call it health insurance, it had to cover that top ten list. There could be copayments and deductibles involved, of course, but the benefits still counted as "covered."

That important list carried with it one more layer underneath: Certain healthcare services, mostly involving preventative screenings and vaccinations, and also (more controversially) birth control, had to be not just covered, but covered with "zero cost sharing," a technical term that many inaccurately rounded up to "free." (It's more like the "free" breakfast at a hotel – you paid for it, but in a different way.)

So while there are many ways to fund home visitation, the simplest is probably to just add it to that list. Do that, and medical providers will suddenly have a strong financial incentive to do aggressive outreach to new parents and generally make the visits happen.

We could even go one step further and attempt to bribe moms-to-be into the healthcare system, as they do in Finland. Facing a high infant mortality rate 75 years ago, the government started handing out cardboard "baby boxes" stuffed with baby clothes and other essentials. The box itself has a mattress bottom that makes it the baby's first crib. While the box and the goodies inside tend to get all the attention, experts credit the drop in the infant mortality rate (now lower than ours) to the fact that getting the box is contingent on making prenatal care appointments and generally developing a close relationship with the medical system, which is what really helps infant health and safety.

This will not be easy. The cost of these services would be absorbed either by everyone who pays taxes, or everyone who pays insurance premiums, depending on how you do it. And of course, people are reluctant to pay more to help poor people they don't know raise kids they feel should have not been conceived in the first place. As advocates for children, we should most emphatically not respond to this grumbling with horror and empathy arguments that appeal only to our side. Instead, we should point out to the skeptics that a few nurse visits for kids is actually much cheaper than a few jail or drug rehab visits for adults. And it may even delay the next pregnancy, leaving the parents with more time to get their act together without help from their fellow taxpayers.

We should also add, given the volatile and corruptible nature of this nation's leadership, that city and state governments may be the first line of defense on this matter, even if national action is more efficient. It is entirely within the realm of the possible for a wealthy city like Seattle to create funding streams to guarantee home visitation to every new parent who is interested. Poorer towns might have to look to a state or county for such things, just as they rely on sheriff's departments and state police forces instead of city cops. But however it works, we know this: the data tell us that investing that money when kids are young will prevent far costlier episodes involving behavioral health programs and child welfare systems.

Idea Two: The early years and the urgent need for universal preschool

Fast forward a bit, and Ethan is now three. Though he doesn't know it yet, he is one of the lucky ones. Deirdre was tipped off to a visitation program, and a visiting nurse was able to identify several problems around the house and gaps in Deirdre's parenting knowledge that could have put Ethan in danger. For example, Deirdre had heard about the discredited home remedy of giving babies a little alcohol to help them sleep, especially during teething. This practice can actually result in everything from vomiting, all the way up to death, but the nurse was able to quash this catastrophe before it began. The nurse also noticed floor cabinets that needed childproofing, and was able to explain how to set that up at minimal cost. And back when Ethan was a newborn, the nurse noticed that Deirdre seemed weepy and overwhelmed several weeks in a row, so she referred her to a therapist and got her help with postpartum depression.

Ethan's treacherous journey to adulthood, however, is just beginning. Deirdre has managed to stamp out obvious physical health hazards from the house, and she can get Ethan to sleep without endangering his health, but as a single mom with a full-time job and not much family support, the need for high-quality educational child care for Ethan was obvious and huge.

Babies absorb enormous amounts of information in the first few years of life. Their brains are flywheels, taking in all sorts of outside stimuli at 100 miles per hour. They look at mobiles, play with interesting toys, and revel in the enthusiastic adult faces coming in close and making all sorts of enriching sounds that they will one day identify as words. They can't really do anything productive, of course, but what they learn in the first few years is a critical foundation on which future careers and relationships are built. (When we tell a partner that "you're so much like your mother" – we're talking about a process that starts here.)

Once they start to talk and have worked out that their personhood is separate in some critical way from mom and dad and the other people around them, what we more conventionally think of as "learning" kicks into high gear. Pre-kindergarten toddlers play a great deal with others, and this is an important basis for all the collaborative relationships they're going to have to navigate in school, and later, the workplace. They also learn basic delayed gratification ("finish your dinner if you want to eat dessert"), behavior control ("we don't hit other people") and elementary reasoning skills ("that car makes a noise, and the big truck makes a louder noise").

We once saw a perfect heartwarming example of this early childhood education at a lunchtime piano recital held at an art museum in a medium-sized western city. A mother had brought her daughter of three or four to the concert, a move that right away pegged them as well-resourced (again using the definition of two parents who probably went to college). The mom walked into the hall, carefully surveyed the scene, then picked a seat next to us for the same reason we had posted up there – it had a direct line of sight to the fingers of the pianist, something that certainly makes those concerts more interesting. It carried the bonus of being close to the front, so the vertically challenged child would not face a wall of bodies.

We can confirm these motivations because she explained every step of the selection process to the child as they sat down. As they settled in, the impressive barrage of parental enrichment continued. With ten minutes to show time, the daughter was quizzed: Did she notice the unusual shape of the grand piano? Did she know why it was shaped like that? Did she understand that plucking short strings produced a high pitched sound while plucking long strings produced a low sound? Could she see from the shape of the piano how it could contain some long strings and some short strings? Would she like to see up close what it looked like inside? Would the nice people sitting next to us, who were conveniently writing a book about childhood, be good enough to save our seats while we go and have a look? (*Ma'am, we would be delighted.*)

This stimulating back-and-forth is how resourced people raise kids. Every one of those interactions builds synapses in the brain and a foundation that kids use to think their way toward health, money, and supportive relationships. We're not understating the case by saying that little conversations about pianos are the building blocks to a healthy and productive life.

Poor kids don't get this treatment nearly enough, sometimes thanks to lack of awareness, but much more frequently, thanks to the time-starved logistics of single parenthood and time consuming jobs that nevertheless leave them only just about managing. A solo parent is, quite simply, going to have to make double the effort to talk to a child that two parents would. Meanwhile, the increased pressures of being the sole breadwinner and the lack of healthy family connections also usually translate into less of this conversational enrichment. And for the same reasons Deirdre didn't recognize obvious hazards around the house, she is probably not going to recognize the urgent need to strike up more engaging conversations, much less have the time, connections, or money to attend recitals and hold forth on the structure and design of musical instruments.

All of that means that by the time Ethan turns five, he will have heard, on average, 30 million fewer words than the girl at the recital. He will have fallen behind on behavior control and reasoning skills as well. TV is often his real babysitter, and that doesn't help the equation one bit. Gaps like this generally get bigger over time, creating a companion self-esteem problem. Kids who get behind tend to stay behind, and a few good chats with a nurse will do only so much to change this.

This is the disease that good preschool (used interchangeably here with *early childhood education*) is meant to cure. You may have heard that all you ever needed to know you learned in kindergarten, and while that is a great book, the title is not literally true. Kindergartners are not blank slates, and kindergarten is no trifling matter. Some kids arrive ready to do the work, and some don't, and preschool is our best bet for a great equalizer.

Preschool is brought up for ridicule sometimes as being glorified daycare, probably because it's a bit of a mental stretch for professionals who do economically productive things all day to see the obvious value in a bunch of three-year-olds playing cooperative games, singing, and doing art projects that always seem to involve dry noodles. They seem to be having altogether too much fun, something few of us readily associate with learning (that's another scandal and another book). And in any event, the line of thinking goes, these are things that could happen at home. Parents are perfectly capable of supervising these activities without getting some institution and tax dollars involved.

These arguments are not entirely without merit. Many parents are capable of doing excellent do-it-yourself early childhood education. (And if that small-but-impressive cadre of homeschooled Harvard graduates is any indication, many could take on later grades as well.) The girl at the recital could probably get by just fine without formal preschool, because she has plenty of the informal kind. (But most likely, she attends the highest quality preschool in town, since her mom has no doubt had time to read all the articles on the importance of such things.)

The insinuation that this reality negates the need for early childhood education is absurd. Good preschool has been shown to shrink the achievement gap, but there is no evidence to suggest that incessant complaining about low-income parenting practices does the same. Besides, we couldn't help but notice that not a few higher income people grousing about new entitlements go to fantastic lengths to get their own kids into great preschools, a high stakes process that almost resembles college admissions. And as for the alleged non seriousness of learning among the under-five set, that's just a matter of walking before you run. Education is not the exclusive domain of well-tenured experts with PhDs conveying complex information to ready minds. Sometimes it's a piece of construction paper, some glue, and a repurposed box of Kraft macaroni and cheese. Laugh all you want: the road to college often starts in the pasta aisle.

But more to the point, while the girl at the concert would probably do fine without preschool, Ethan may have big problems. When we were busy listening to Chopin, he was most likely watching TV or biding his time in a daycare that didn't feed his brain much. Lots of kids out there are born into families that can't afford to send them to preschool or don't have the skills or the time to pull off some homeschool arrangement. Paradoxically enough, they are both the kids who are least likely to go to preschool, and the kids who need it the most.

That's why a family-friendly city will offer universal preschool starting at age three, or ideally even younger. It wouldn't be compulsory, but any child could enroll regardless of the family's ability to pay, just like the K-12 system. Exactly where and how this happens could take many different forms. We could just give school districts some extra money and tell them to add a couple of extra grades before kindergarten. We could also contract out the services by getting existing private preschools to expand.

Which method is best? We don't have an opinion on this. So long as every kid like Ethan gets the sort of education that helps him play in the same ballpark with Recital Girl by kindergarten, we're okay with it. He needs to be in an environment full of words and challenges and opportunities to learn how to interact with others, because that's the basis of a productive life, and he won't get it unless we make it happen for him.

This may sound intuitive enough, and it may resonate well with your own experience, no matter which side of the tracks you grew up on. But as usual with new ideas that involve spending money, there is something of a backlash against the idea that preschool is effective at closing this achievement gap. In fact, the whole debate seems to vaguely resemble the global warming controversy: The evidence is very clear that kids who attend preschool are more ready for kindergarten. The effect is most evident for low-income kids. Other studies say that particular ways of doing early childhood education are more effective than some alternatives. All in all, it's a big soup of chatter that is hard for laity to digest.

If you wish to become an expert in the scientific literature covering these matters, there are plenty of other books out there that will help you do that. Here, we'll just share with you the reasons why we are vehemently in favor of universal preschool, despite the overblown controversy. First, most of the evidence points to it being very effective in helping kids like Ethan close the gap on his wealthy peers. Second, the benefits of well-trained adults guiding children toward developing their own brains and vocabularies are obvious and intuitive and can be seen even at casual piano recitals. If we take as a given that preschool can replicate that sort of interaction, albeit with the normal challenges of scaling up to a group/institutional model, then the benefits are likewise obvious and intuitive, especially when we know they're not available at home. It's going to take a heck of a lot of contrary evidence to convince us otherwise, and right now that evidence doesn't exist.

The third reason to support universal preschool approaches the question from a risk-management perspective. Simply put, we don't have much to lose by putting a bunch of kids in preschool, but if failing to do so results in those kids making less money, paying less in tax, and taking more out of the welfare system, then we stand to lose a lot.

Still, it's probably a good idea to listen carefully to critics on this matter, because they may tell us something about how best to do preschool in general, and what methods most effectively get kids like Ethan where they need to go. By and large, people studying this issue are trying to be constructive. There may be a global fossil fuel lobby working hard to obscure the science on global warming, but we're not aware of any such corollary force acting in the shadows against preschool.

Whatever the case, we should proactively evaluate these efforts early and often, something we think the continuous quality improvement unit in the child welfare department would be great at, probably in conjunction with school districts or education regulators or public health officials. We need good data to see how these efforts are all going, and we need to see a rolling estimate of the number of three and four-year-olds in the state, along with the number of them enrolled in preschool. Progress could be tracked by studying how prepared students are to take on kindergarten.

We could even identify a few control groups of kids that didn't go to preschool and check in with them every year for a few decades, comparing their progress to that of the kids that enrolled. We might even be able to extrapolate whether the program is paying for itself by delivering increased productivity gains and tax revenue from the higher paying jobs the kids eventually land. That would give us some valuable local data that could be put up for all to see, hopefully paired with headlines like "In 400 percent return, county rakes in $46 million from preschool gains." The reporting may tell us that what we're doing is working, which will certainly be nice to know. And it may tell us that what we're doing is not working, which is valuable too.

We should also point out here that while we've bent over backwards to address the critics, this is hardly a revolutionary or partisan issue, and we won't have to reinvent any wheels. Nearly every state already has publicly-funded preschool, though it is often targeted only at low-income kids and generally fails to enroll enough of them. Nationally, only about one quarter of four-year-olds are in state preschool.

But a few states have quietly made this a priority and seen great results. In Oklahoma, about 75 percent of four-years-olds are enrolled. The notorious swing state of Florida is close to 80 percent. And Washington D.C., one of the most reliably liberal jurisdictions in the country, is at 94 percent. Meanwhile, Alabama and Delaware are political opposites, but both languish in the mid-single digits. Figuring this out is basically a matter of connecting a few dots and writing a check, and states all over the political spectrum have shown they can do it.

In fact, America has already shown it can do it, because we've done it before. About 100 years ago, public education basically stopped at 8th grade, but we changed that to adapt to a new modern reality. High school is universal, and more and more people are going to college. Today, it's time to get going again.

Bottom line: Early childhood education can play an important role in reducing the prevalence of ACEs. Not only does it steer kids clear of destructive behaviors, beating a path toward great jobs and, one day, their own healthy families, but the institution itself can be a great way for other pairs of eyes to screen out problems and do something about them before it's too late.

Idea Three: Youth mentoring, just a phone call away

Let's continue our optimistic narrative of Ethan's life and assume that he not only got good home visitation, but also went to a capably managed preschool and arrived at kindergarten more-or-less ready for prime time. He was not top of his class, to be sure. Some kids arrived already a couple of grades ahead in reading and math (looking at you, Recital Girl), but Ethan was a respectable average. Considering where he came from, this counted as way ahead of the game. Through elementary school, he woke up every morning, went to school, ate the free breakfast and lunch that his poverty-stricken household of two easily qualified for, and went home.

For six or seven hours per day, Ethan was surrounded by reasonably good influences and got two squares out of the deal. Deirdre, for her part, kept working a series of low-paying jobs, and while she was personally a mess, she managed to maintain some degree of stability. Nobody would wish for such a childhood, but those who looked at the context would probably conclude that it could have been much worse.

But Ethan is now nine, and there is trouble ahead. Nothing cataclysmic, thank goodness, though plenty of kids like Ethan face that. This trouble is just the normal pain of growing up, plus the additional pain of not having much of a support network or a dad. Between the stress of growing bodies and developing brains, a lack of wisdom from a long life full of experiences, prominent hormonal imbalances, and the sudden critical nature of romantic affairs, childhood is always a process of walking through a minefield. In resourced families, there are people who can keep close tabs and steer you away from the mines, or at least rush in and patch you up when something explodes. Low-income families, however, are much more alone on this front.

For those of us who have put a few years between ourselves and elementary school, it is easy to forget how inevitable and eternal that youthful routine felt. Summer vacations lasted an unfathomable three months, but 12 years of this, plus preschool, followed by whatever this much-hyped college business turned out to be, was too much to really process. We all talked about the future and what we would be when we grew up, and we meant it, as hilariously naive as it sounds in retrospect. The adults clucked approvingly of our ambitious career selection, but at the same time it all seemed very far away.

We're taking this reminiscing detour to make the point that it is very easy to get tunnel vision in childhood, and it can feel pretty claustrophobic. You strain to branch out, to see the world beyond your tiny orbit, to become yourself, and this is actually a very healthy thing often slandered as mere rebellion. Like Luke Skywalker, you look around for a window into the big unknown, but from the soft prison that is childhood, these things are hard to find.

Good youth mentors take on a sort of Obi-Wan Kenobi role, minus all the violence and interstellar travel. They can throw a psychological lifeline to kids in this tense and stressful situation. They come from the brave new world of Your Future bearing glad tidings of what life is like when you do not live under mom's roof. They are exhibits of the sweet freedom to come, but also models of how to relish it with responsibility and ethics. On their best days, they understand you in ways that mom (or your adoptive aunt and uncle) can't.

Being a single mother is not for the faint of heart. Those raising boys like Ethan are in a particularly tough spot when it comes to – and we assure you this is the proper scientific term – guy stuff. Little boys like to do strange things like play catch for hour after hour in the park and tell jokes involving gross noises that only little boys or people who were once little boys can possibly appreciate. Older boys often enjoy watching movies replete with comic violence, and comparing notes about attraction with someone other than mom. Surrounded by women, they are often not sure what it means to be a man. They are also capable of crazy or sometimes scary behaviors that can be particularly perplexing to someone who was never, say, a 16-year-old boy.

We generally talk about youth mentoring as if it were a nice, pleasant, anodyne thing to do. Hang out with some kid and play board games or do crafts a couple of times per month, and in exchange you will bubble over with good vibes for having made an "impact." But this understates the case. Youth mentors save lives.

Not in obvious ways, of course, and not often literally, and not every time. But youth mentors can serve as guardrails for life. On their best days, they are anchors of stability in an unsettled world. They are windows that look out onto the vast possibilities of life after the parental police state. They are people we wish to become. They are a combination of coach and therapist and confidant. They are givers of occasional advice, and while it may not sink in right away, it often sticks in the long term somehow. Often, this advice isn't even spoken: The mere presence of a stable adult who maintains healthy relationships with their peers and holds down a good job stands as a secular version of Saint Francis's admonishment to preach the gospel every day, and to use words when necessary.

There's one more annoying detail about the concept of youth mentoring in the popular imagination. Somehow, we have come to think of it as something that is done for the benefit of poor children. While this is not untrue, it negates the reality that kids from resourced households benefit greatly from youth mentoring – we just don't call it that.

Perhaps you had, all things considered, a great childhood. Odds are good it was still marked by intense confusion, stress, and insecurity. School is awful, parents are clueless and mean, romantic relationships are scary, life is just so intense, and that's the best case scenario. What made it better, or at least tolerable? Youth mentors by another name.

Maybe it was the family across the street that adopted you for entire weekends so you could get away from your own and imagine the vast possibilities of life. Maybe it was an aunt or uncle to whom you could tell secrets, or maybe they just represented some ideal that you didn't see at home and found comforting. Maybe it was a good teacher. Maybe some family friends moved to another state then arranged for you to come visit and do grunt work on their home construction project, opening up further possibilities. These are just a few of the experiences and relationships we have had personally, and we shudder to think of what life would have been like without them.

DOM'S JOURNAL
For years, I traveled the country on a breakneck schedule, talking about child welfare in general while evangelizing for youth mentoring in particular. While I didn't work for Big Brothers Big Sisters, I would still happily tell anyone who would listen that volunteering with them was one of the best things a person could possibly do.

The "come-to-Jesus" moment about my own lack of volunteering was probably inevitable. After some interior back and forth, I took the plunge.

I ended up being matched with a shy 14-year-old who first appeared in an oversize dark sweatshirt that barely revealed the bottom half his face. He was an insightful young man with a quiet keen intellect. And spending time with him has been one of the greatest experiences of my life. We took long strolls through Santa Fe on Saturday afternoons, having colorful conversations about his growing up in rural New Mexico, sharing a house with five siblings, and responding to the attention of girls. We visited a college of design, library, and art galleries. We both shared a love of tech and scary movies. I was also able to help with his school work, and learned a lot about how the system can let a brilliant young person (with high marks in math and engineering) struggle with the other topics without so much as a parent-teacher conference initiated.

Parents, meanwhile, are in the thick of the drama, cajoling, prodding, and fighting good sense and character into their kids. But nobody was born knowing how to do this. Happy adolescents are all alike, to mangle some wisdom of Tolstoy, but unhappy adolescents are unhappy in their own individual ways. Their antics are often irrational, irritating, and downright insane. It's easy to get overwhelmed, and not a few parents of mentored youth have made discreet phone calls to the mentors wondering how the hell they are supposed to manage the latest crisis, and they've gotten a lot out of those talks.

Kids like Ethan and parents like Deirdre are not guaranteed those lifelines. They are not baked into the cake that is their family life and social circumstances. Those who grew up in resourced families with lots of youth mentors have no idea what they would have done without them, and those who have successfully parented a child have no idea what they would have done without those with whom they were able to compare notes. Our job is to take heed and make sure that no kid or parent has to find out what life is like in that mentorless void.

This is no pipe dream. We have it in our power to make sure that every kid like Ethan has a mentor. We should do better at screening for ACEs in schools, and we should make sure teachers and other faculty are formally trained to spot danger signs, but identifying the kids who need mentors is not rocket science. Give a teacher a cocktail napkin and they could write down a list of names for you right now without thinking much about it.

We also know that youth mentoring works. Kids who participate are less likely to use drugs, less likely to abuse alcohol, less likely to skip school, and they even get a slight bump in GPA out of the deal. It is a great way to ameliorate the effects of adverse childhood experiences, as well as reduce the likelihood that they will be passed to the next generation.

But just like every other prescription for a family-friendly city, the goal is much simpler than the actual path to victory. The good news is that most communities have some kind of mentoring program on which to build (often through that gold standard of organizations, Big Brothers Big Sisters). The bad news is that we're not aware of any community that has met its demand. There is likely a shortage of mentors, a problem that would be even greater if they had sufficient outreach power to make sure every parent, teacher, pastor, and pediatrician knew the program existed and stood ready to send families their way. The shortage is particularly acute with male mentors.

The story will be different in every state, every county, and every city, which is where good data collection comes in. As with most of what we've been discussing in this book, the first step is to assess the problem thoroughly, something that becomes the basis for planning, action, and later, finding out if what happened actually worked. Lucky for us, there aren't too many metrics to gather. (The continuous quality improvement staff at a large youth development non-profit agency could do it, and share the results quarterly on social media.)

Basically we need to take a community and figure out how many kids there are between six and 18 years old, which is the age range that Big Brothers Big Sisters deals with and seems like a good place to start. From there, we could use some combination of census poverty stats, childhood poverty numbers, or free and reduced lunch numbers to come up with a decent ballpark percentage of the total youth population that we should be targeting. As always, these numbers go up on the web, preferably on a colorful and intuitive chart.

Next we measure the supply, which should be available from whatever other agency does youth mentoring in your community. Get them on the phone and see if they'll tell you how many youths they currently work with and what their waiting list looks like, especially when broken down by gender. They might even tell you about their recruiting strategy and give you some clues as to what might help get more mentors on board and more kids enrolled. All of this information also goes up on the web. (Or, if you happen to have lots of money, we've long thought it would be cool to put up digital billboards around a town that show the real-time number of how many kids are on the waiting list, but that's some serious extra credit.)

With those numbers, you'll know how much work your community has cut out for it. You may need to focus on outreach to families, or you may need to focus on mentor recruitment, or maybe both. But once you know the shape and size of the problem, you can begin to plan the attack.

The bottom line: A caring, compassionate, and communicative mentor and mentee can form a trusting and stable non-parent relationship, a critical component of all kid's lives, but one that is all-too-often missing. We know it can transform lives for the better, and we have the data to prove it.

With all this money and talent, what's really keeping us from building a safer America?

Let's say the magic wand has already been waved. With a flick of the wrist and an abracadabra, we have built a better mental health care system, made sure child welfare departments run like Swiss watches, and implemented a full array of parental supports, early childhood programs, and youth mentorship opportunities. The few who are not accessing these services are in that place only because they have repeatedly turned down the invitation.

So, are we there yet? Is this the promised land where it is all but impossible for kids like Anna to end up in the city morgue?

Not quite. We're confident that implementing the agenda described up to this point in the book would take a huge bite out of the problem – maybe 80 percent in total. But if we truly wish to eradicate adverse childhood experiences, we've got a few more things to check off the list. Okay a lot of things. Your economic destiny in the United States, a country we tell ourselves is a meritocracy, still largely depends on what zip code you happen to be born into, even with good mentoring, preschool, and home visitation. Your ability to escape the negative effects of ACEs is no different, and that has to change. If we truly want to address ACEs, we'll need to tackle seven key service areas outlined below with ferocity and passion.

NOTE: We realize that we're about to go from advocating three relatively simple proposals that just seek to make universal a few existing programs that are themselves relatively cheap and bipartisan, to advocating for sweeping reforms that would fundamentally remake American society. We're doing this for a couple of reasons – (1) We don't mind aiming high, and (2) we think it's important to point out that a lot of big nebulous challenges actually have a big impact on kids in a non-intuitive way.

Challenge 1: Health Care

We've spent plenty of time on mental health care, but traditional healthcare and dental are important here too. Simply put, untreated or poorly treated health or dental ailments can drag down school performance, strain relationships, and generally stand in the way of a good life for kids. Our best bet for fighting this is easy access to a quality health care system at an affordable price (which will, for some people, be $0). We need not become the United Kingdom – where everything is free at the point of service – but we should make sure that parents don't skip their kid's medical treatment because they can't afford it. Comprehensive health care also includes comprehensive reproductive health care, which means healthier kids, and happier, better-prepared parents. Win win.

Challenge 2: Housing

Housing affordability is a challenge that has been with us for a long time, and there are many different strategies out there for addressing it. We won't spend much time on those, but we will point out that it's not in anybody's interest to have lots of people spending a quarter or half of their income on housing. It just puts lots of families in an economic pressure cooker that can increase the likelihood of ACEs and relegate them to substandard units in the worst neighborhoods, while making it all the harder to flee an abusive relationship. Both the libertarian types and European socialists have ideas for fixing this, but we don't have an opinion on which should be deployed, so long as it works (and no one is left homeless).

Challenge 3: Education and Family-Centered Schools

Lots of schools in under-resourced areas are strapped for cash because the systems are funded by local property taxes. This means they have a harder time affording the best teaching talent, which doesn't make the situation any better. Schools can be a key, frontline defense against ACEs, but only if they have the money and the know-how to do the job. Schools are the one place that even kids in the most dire of circumstances somehow get to most of the time. The more services we can pack into schools, after school and summer programs, mentoring programs, social workers, case managers, employment centers, medical, reproductive, and behavioral health services, on site tutoring, the better. As we said in the previous chapter, if we put all of these services in a place that kids are going anyway, they are far more likely to take advantage of them. And if we address the underlying root causes of poor school performance in low income neighborhoods, test scores, attendance rates, and graduation rates will get better, and as an added bonus kids will be safer and healthier.

Challenge 4: Job Training and Living Wage Jobs

Living wage jobs create stable families. Having money just makes it easier to raise kids, afford medical care, and achieve the stability that you need to form good supportive relationships. Whether this is accomplished by a high minimum wage, make-work programs, a wage subsidy, a universal basic income, or some free-market solution we have yet to see comprehensively work in the real world, we again don't care. If the result is Deirdre with a living wage, that means Ethan is well cared for. More living wage jobs means fewer ACEs.

Challenge 5: Hunger

With millions of our fellow Americans on food stamps, and food pantries being the fixtures of communities that they are, it seems inconceivable that kids in our country suffer from hunger. And in fact, the reality on the ground is probably less dramatic than those who make grand pronouncements about "one in five" kids suffering from hunger would have us believe. Are lots of kids starving to death out there? No. But plenty of children live in households where money is so tight that parents have a hard time picking up where food stamps leave off. (Your state student surveys will most likely tell you how many kids are experiencing hunger monthly, and this is a data point every ACEs prevention program needs to be on top of.) That can translate into skipping meals or eating poorly balanced meals. And even if there's a food pantry that stands ready to help, it's not guaranteed that mom or dad will have the logistical capacity to pick up the groceries. Meanwhile, we throw away about 40 percent of our food due to spoilage or because it didn't look quite as appetizing when we got home from the store. Call us crazy, but it seems like some logistical solutions could be found here that wouldn't be very expensive. That, or we can pay for the consequences of hungry kids later.

Challenge 6: Transportation

America is a pretty car-centric nation, and this can mean extreme difficulty going to the grocery store or work for those with limited or no automobile access. While many transit systems run like tops, others are very inefficient, having been relegated to some talent-challenged dark corner of city government with all the other services for poor undesirables. What does this have to do with ACEs? Everything. When we talk about beating an easy path to healthy food in real grocery stores, better jobs, and good preschools, that path is often traversed by public transit. Luckily, transportation is pretty cheap, and we're already pretty good at it (school bus networks are very impressive, after all). And the coming revolution of autonomous vehicles could well make it all easier.

Challenge 7: Behavioral Health Care

We just spent the previous chapter explaining why this is vital. We won't be healing and preventing childhood trauma and maltreatment without a robust behavioral healthcare system in every community. (Yes, we have our work cut out for us.)

And completing the list of the top ten "surviving and thriving" family services already mentioned, we have: **Challenge 8: Parent supports; Challenge 9: Early childhood learning programs; Challenge 10: Youth mentoring.**

Piercing the power of the zip code

There will always be less-than-desirable zip codes in the United States. Some will have a few more potholes in the roads, more above-ground power lines instead of the aesthetically pleasing underground variety, and bad luck of the draw when it comes to scenery. There are natural advantages to consider as well – the Port of Seattle is much more attractive for shipping and its associated higher-paying jobs than the Port of Portland, but it's actually geography at work there, not a public policy failure.

The point here is not to advocate for some dystopian sci-fi scheme where everyone's living standards are equalized and big brother or an android nanny determines our destiny. The point is merely to say that we cannot afford the lost economic productivity, tax revenue, and increased addiction and crime that neglecting the kids in our less attractive zip codes would produce. So of course, throw them the obvious and relatively inexpensive lifelines like nurse visitation, preschool, and youth mentoring, and that will help a lot. Then work on food, healthcare, housing, transport, jobs, and schools, and pretty soon, those neighborhoods are no longer the festering environments of hopelessness and dysfunction. They probably won't become 90210, but so long as the kids are alright, America will be too.

_____

Chapter Eight

There's an app for that (maybe): Healthy kids and the promises and perils of technology

Anna's Story

One of many factors behind Anna's unfortunate return to her mother was technology. Anna's story was documented, of course, but that data file (and various paper files), had to be repeatedly tracked down, year after year, by new staffers thrown against a less-than-user-friendly data system. That sort of system makes knowledge gaps caused by human error (not finding the right file needle in the file haystack) very possible, which is one of the factors that may have contributed to Anna's fate. But if we invest in the right software, technology, and staffing, it need not be this way. For child maltreatment and ACEs, the right tracking systems (and a plethora of other tech) are going to be vital if we really intend to do coordinated prevention work.

TWENTY YEARS AGO, should you have felt the need to sell your lawnmower, you would likely have phoned up a newspaper, and, for a few bucks, dictated a classified ad out to a human. In smaller towns, you might have even visited the newspaper's headquarters and filled out a form, chatting with an amiable receptionist as you wrote.

The receptionist would take this information to some other human, who would assemble your classified ad, along with perhaps hundreds of others. At the same time, still other humans delivered massive rolls of shredded and compressed tree pulp to a manufacturing plant nearby. There, more humans would receive the collection of ads, then deploy a massive and noisy machine (along with the tree pulp and large vats of ink) to create a remarkable facsimile of those ads. Other humans would physically deliver these "papers" to a large fraction of front porches in the area, where they could be read alongside breakfast and later redeployed to pack away wine glasses for moving day.

It was a real Rube Goldberg machine, but at the end of the day, assuming reasonably good condition and a fair price, you probably sold that lawnmower.

Today, you can still sell that lawnmower, but you'll do so on Craigslist. And if you're looking to sell a house, a car, or recruit for a job, you'll probably do it with an app or website that traces its founding concept back to that company.

Thanks to these firms, the whole selling process has taken a turn for the awesome. Suddenly, there is limitless space to describe every contour of the lawnmower (no coded abbreviations necessary), and you can upload more pictures than any reasonable person would ever want to look at. Best of all, it's free or close to it, and instantaneous. You need not leave your house, and once you sell, you can take the ad down right away, so there's no need to field repeated calls about whether the sold item is still available.

All it took to revolutionize the classified ad world was a little technology: Some computers, both the handheld and desktop variety, and some wires or signals to connect them. The word "efficient" doesn't even begin to describe the results. Once upon a time, classified ad revenue from one medium-sized newspaper you've never heard of might have supported dozens of employees, who all worked hard to maintain a clunky, inefficient, time-consuming, hard-to-use system that got your lawnmower sold. Today, Craigslist takes the place of that operation, and many hundreds of thousands more all over the world, while being run by a laughably small group of about 40 people.

That, in a nutshell, is the seductive allure of technology. It comes along and sweeps a problem off its feet, and seemingly without effort, elegantly solves whatever used to ail society. Life is hard, but once in a while technology just drops a freebie out from the sky (or the cloud), and suddenly it's a lot easier to sell a lawnmower, or hail a taxi, or book a room.

But far from settling for being merely easy to use, those who sell technology go to great lengths to project wildly attractive coolness about the whole business. The interfaces are utilitarian, yes, but they are also beautiful (the notable exception-that-proves-the-rule is Craigslist). This or that new app does not grow, it disrupts. They do not change an industry, but rather revolutionize.

There is technical talent at play, to be sure, but that demigod-of-the-business Steve Jobs was also a hell of a showman, complete with a personality cult that survives to this day, and we were all happy to go along for the ride. Our society throws billions into dubious tech ventures bound for failure. Tech even had its own bubble, which is another word for contraction in the face of irrational exuberance that just got found out. The industry does some neat tricks, then lays on the messianic sales job pretty hard.

Don't get us wrong: we love technology. When the history of this era is written 100 years hence, we wouldn't be surprised if the conclusion comes down on the side of Craigslist as a net plus for society. We're not saying you should ditch Uber and go back to traditional taxis or somehow not admire the design of the latest Apple product. We are, however, saying that a sober assessment of technology's promise is in order, especially when it comes to a knotty social issue like ACEs. We should tread carefully, because getting swept off our feet and distracted by an industry whose interests, financial and otherwise, don't necessarily align with America's kids, won't help the cause one bit.

Still, we can imagine a long list of fascinating ways that technology – both the kind we have now and the kind that they say is just around the corner – could potentially help our kids avoid and recover more efficiently from ACEs.

Artificially intelligent coaches/therapists: We mentioned this in a previous chapter, but consider this anyway: Instead of paying $90/hour to someone with years of training, maybe future citizens in need of talk therapy could converse with a really intuitive, expertly designed, trauma-informed chatbot (one that knew when it was in over its little artificial head and would refer you to a behavioral health care human). Even if it's only half as good as a well-trained human, it would be extremely cost effective. The possibilities are profound.

Mapping and visualization: One reason the problems we've elaborated in this book remain unsolved is that we as a society have a hard time understanding them. But thanks to mapping software, democratized graphic design, and troves of digitized data, illustrating those problems has never been easier and will only get more so. As we said elsewhere in these pages, the first step is admitting you have a problem, but even before that you have to see it.

On that subject: Mapping doesn't have to be a matter of some experts collecting and presenting information in a beautiful way – it can actually be a collaborative project. The New Mexico Department of Transportation recently launched a project where bicyclists can get online and attach comments to a map of state bicycle routes. It's the sort of feedback that used to require a big meeting and paper, but it now happens from the convenience of everybody's home. The same thing could be used to monitor and comment on the infrastructure that is supposed to help kids.

Institutional tracking software: This is where Silicon Valley really shines. Thousands of people labor every day over software packages that basically promise nothing more than the ability to efficiently keep track of stuff (though they will of course not explain it so simply). It's the real secret to success for the likes of FedEx and Wal-Mart and Amazon, because it means they be maximally productive with the least amount of effort/money. Good tracking software is easy to use, shows you what is going on with (sometimes downright beautiful) visualizations, and generally causes you to wonder how the hell you ever got by without it. (Hint: We used to call up taxi dispatchers and hope a car showed up at some point.) State and local bureaucracies in charge of tracking kids and parents could use this software to do their jobs much more efficiently, and, in turn, help more kids.

Attitude adjustment: Though they can come off as arrogant little know-it-alls, what with their incessant talk of disruption, block chains, and the internet of things, we do, as a general rule, like how the tech industry thinks. They've got these amazing tools at their disposal that they themselves are just beginning to understand (See Zuckerberg, Mark – 2016 election), and they just sort of maraud about the world trying to fix things and make money. What if that sort of talent, venture capital backing, and unflinching experimentation were turned loose on the problems faced by our kids? The answer: Who knows, but we enjoy thinking about it sometimes while wistfully looking out toward the horizon.

Tempered enthusiasm

And the list could go on. So yes, our technological future may also hold great promise for the fight against childhood trauma and maltreatment. But before we go overboard, there are a few reasons to exercise caution.

First, these technologies may well cause new problems for our kids as they solve other things. There's some evidence that social media leads to increased anxiety in children, since they feel pressured to measure up against the perfectly curated non-reality in the Facebook newsfeed, where everyone is always happy, traveling somewhere, or eating something delicious. Bullies have always been around, but now they have fancy new technological venues to pursue their predations. To the extent that technology takes us away from face-to-face communities, it leaves vulnerable those relationships with friends and family that function as a kind of social insurance against ACEs. And as technology reshapes the labor markets, it creates economic losers whose kids are more vulnerable to ACEs.

Again, this is not to say that technology is bad – just that it can be a double edged sword, and it would be in poor taste to obsess about the sheer awesomeness of it all while ignoring the problems it creates, even if they're smaller and more manageable than the original problem.

Our second reason for caution relates to the nature of the alleged miracles that technology has worked. Simply put, there's reason to be awestruck, but there's also reason to see those victories as limited, because the problems they solved were not that challenging in the first place.

All over the United States (and the world), for example, classified ads efficiently matched up willing sellers of lawnmowers with willing buyers. The system featured some considerable friction (pulped and compressed trees, intricate machinery, etc.) and some time delays (the trip to the newspaper office, publication prep, delivery time), but on the whole, it worked pretty well. ACEs are a national scandal right now, as everyone who pays the slightest attention to the issue already knows, but nobody in 1975 considered the allegedly laborious process of paying five bucks and chatting with a friendly newspaper receptionist to be a fundamentally tragic process. It wasn't exactly efficient in our modern eyes, but again, it worked, and also paid for the reporter in the newsroom to attend city council meetings and put bothersome questions to politicians who were thus a little more honest in their everyday dealings.

Enter Craigslist, and now the whole process is more efficient and basically free. But they didn't fundamentally change anything. Before, newspapers aggregated classified ads and then published them. Craigslist does the same thing, but uses new tools. Airbnb was not the first service to aggregate rooms for rent, Amazon was not the first flea market, and Uber was not the first taxi dispatcher. They all just used new and fascinating tools to speed things up and make life easier for people interacting with the service, replacing something that was working well with something that worked even better.

We shouldn't hold our breath that technology will solve ACEs for the simple reason that there is not currently a well-functioning system to digitize and make faster. The prescription instead calls for systematic change – things like getting nurses into the homes of all newborn babies, universal preschool, and a big brother or big sister for all kids who need one. It calls for politicians to give a damn where they didn't before, and for their constituents to make them give a damn. And it calls for several government departments to act as though the enlightenment happened and they're on board with it.

These are not things that can be packaged into an app, even if there was some obvious profit motive to be found. Present someone with the option to do something easier and cheaper from the comfort of home and without making any phone calls, and they'll do it, which is why Craigslist is a hit. But fighting ACEs will take money we'd rather not spend, time we'd rather not devote, and a campaign to change minds that would rather not change. It's like the difference between being offered a delicious dessert and being asked to cook an elaborate four-course meal from scratch. There is not as of yet a good app to make sure every baby gets a good start in life. That will take political pressure, a willingness to get out there and change hearts and minds in a saturated media landscape, and the ability to say yes to being a youth mentor.

So by all means, use every piece of cool technology at your disposal. It may well make your life and work a little easier, but it won't negate the need for elbow grease. The tech companies make everything look so smooth and efficient, but that's because next to ACEs, their job is easy.

Chapter Nine

Get the data and make a plan: Why we all live in Santa Fe, New Mexico

Anna's Story

When Anna died after having been in state custody so many times, the child welfare department performed something called a Child Fatality Review. This review is designed to better understand what went wrong and how to fix it. But for these post-mortem processes to be of any help at all, they need to do more. Something can always be done to prevent this sort of thing from happening, even if it has nothing to do with state or local government as it is currently constructed. A fatality report with clear, evidence-based recommendations for new protocols, policies, and programs, running to a national level if need be, would go a long way – especially since it would be able to seize on the spotlight created by the media frenzy that surrounds a child's death. Anna's story need not be repeated if we learn from it.

SANTA FE, NEW MEXICO is one of those cities that makes you play by its own very pleasant set of rules. There's no street grid, for one thing, and the roads tend to meander about like they do in London. The adobe-style buildings all look very different from what you're used to elsewhere else in the United States. The New Mexican food is different, too – more color, more spice, and there's probably a painting on the restaurant wall involving some deep blue and a touch of bright red you don't see very often. Many of the stoplights are, for some reason, horizontal instead of vertical. The climate is dry and rustic feeling. It is both inviting and not at all like where you are from, yet everyone speaks English and accepts American currency, making it the ideal location to deposit some of your hard-earned travel budget. Heck, they even call it the City Different. It is what it is, and you just have to deal with it, but luckily you don't really mind. You visit, have some unique experiences, get outside your routine while staying inside your comfort zone, and leave, clutching some gorgeous piece of art, feeling quite accomplished, and ready to recommend the place to your friends.

Those of us who live in Santa Fe are accustomed to shuttling visitors around town and observing in them this happy cycle of wonder, delight, and contentment. It's great sublime fun, especially on one of those crisp summer evenings when the sun bounces off the Sangre de Cristo mountains just so and the air is still fresh from an afternoon rainstorm. Residents, whether they trace their roots back to before the Spanish settlers or to a Southwest Airlines flight in 2014, take an unusual loving pride in their home.

This side of Santa Fe is real, not just something we cook up for the tourists. We have great experiences like this ourselves even after you head back to the airport. Yet we also know there's more to it than that. There is another part of town where we didn't take you.

In the shadows of Santa Fe's beautiful churches, under those stunning mountainous panoramas, random acts of childhood adversity take place daily, and by the thousands. Within smelling distance of the city's great restaurants, there are low profile cases of neglect and abuse. The occasional child murders are just the tip of the spear: Awful, to be sure, but they didn't get there by themselves. The rest of the spear is a state child poverty rate of 30 percent, the highest in the nation. About 60 percent of New Mexican kids are not in preschool. And 41 percent of our kids live in single parent families. Not coincidentally, the state is also an economic basket case, the brisk Santa Fe tourist business and small slice of Permian Basin oil to the southeast notwithstanding.

Data immunity

But this is old news. Whenever the Annie E. Casey Foundation's Kids Count Survey reveals, yet again, that NM is 49th for being the most unsafe state to be a child, we roll our eyes and say, "well at least this year we aren't 50th." Cynical wags who have seen this movie before will add some assurance that our brilliant leaders will do their best to wrest the crown from Mississippi by this time next year.

Whether you're John Q. Public or an unreconstructed data nerd, you're accustomed to seeing this stuff. Our media outlets, after all, do a dutiful job of publishing the stats regularly. If we failed as an electorate to notice that, we certainly paid attention to a 2016 TV advertising campaign in which a Catholic health organization deftly satirized state tourism ad campaigns while highlighting the bad numbers. "This is New Mexico," the friendly narrator told us as scenic vistas undulated across the screen, "where we celebrate our unique cuisine, and turn a blind eye to our hungry children."

Another piece of old news is that our institutions do not seem to understand that with the right tools, we might be able to make a dent in some of these numbers. We once worked right next to the domestic violence unit of the state's child welfare system, and were talking to them about how to use their treasure trove of data to a useful end. Much could be learned, we reckoned, from the domestic violence shelter clients' use of mental health care services, recovery services, job training, and more. How long do they stay at shelters, and how often do they return? We also asked to track data to tell us about the success rate of the groups for domestic violence offenders.

Their data could be used to figure out what's working and what's not, allowing us to do more of one and less of the other. That translates into less violence, happier childhoods, more economic productivity, and a better quality of life for everyone, which certainly takes the edge off those stressful days at the office.

It was not to be. "That data system is only for invoicing purposes, not for data analysis," the domestic violence unit supervisor said. We countered with, "Yes, but you are sitting on incredibly important data." She didn't agree. It went downhill from there.

A city of extremes

We're tired of it, but we're not alone. Every state has nice towns like Santa Fe that also feature a rough underbelly where you would not want to grow up. And we're not alone when it comes to hapless governments that seem to think their mission in life isn't to solve real problems, but to prevent the employees from buying too many paper clips. The goal appears to be a skin-deep impression of a functioning agency. Hardly anybody out there lives in a community with a comprehensive plan to address childhood trauma. No matter where your state appears on those child well-being lists, you have the same problems. We may be an extreme case here, but in many ways, you too live in Santa Fe.

Many will argue we can't prevent ACEs. Here's why they're wrong.

We've discussed many problems in this book: Entrenched bureaucracy, lack of commitment to data-informed planning and action, and an apathetic public that parachutes into the conversation only when major disaster strikes and then only long enough to label a few people as monsters.

The problems we face in arriving at that shining city on the hill we've described in these pages will not be easy to overcome. They're hard to conceptualize, hard to explain, and are often expensive to solve, at least in the short term. That new overpass alleviates traffic congestion right after the ribbon cutting, and it's fun to build and look at, but a multi-pronged push toward improving kids' lives through harm reduction isn't nearly as satisfying. To most outside observers, a social worker with a proper caseload who is able to help people looks about the same as a social worker with an outrageous caseload who is unable to help people. New bridges are way more interesting than new procedures for how to refer kids to psychologists.

Change is never easy. It comes in time-consuming stages, and often involves steps back. Social organisms called individual humans operate one way, and social organisms called schools, behavioral health experts, and legislatures all have their own unique proclivities, too. The solutions to all the problems illustrated in this book are hiding in plain sight, but with a little effort, we can see them and solve them.

We take a certain comfort in knowing that at the end of the day, there's no disputing that it can be done. This is no moon shot, no World War II, no vast uncertainty into which we must throw ourselves. We know what works, and we know it's just a long series of procedural tweaks, some budget adjustments, and a few more major reforms to get there. It wouldn't even be that expensive (and in fact might well save money, not to mention decades of collective emotional pain), and will surely promote quality of life. We built an education system that takes students through 12 grades, and there's no reason we can't add a couple more at the beginning, then add in a wellness center that can treat emotional trauma, address a strained muscle, and provide birth control. If we can make the buses run on time in a transparent way, we can do the same for child welfare departments, public health departments and education systems. We already field teams of nurses in hospitals and clinics, and there's no reason we can't send them out to the homes of newborn babies as well.

When we all commit to eradicating adverse childhood experiences, we'll end this never-ending trauma. We wrote this book for the general public, because they need to know what's happening, and they need to channel their outrage in a way that pressures all the institutions we pay for into making the end of trauma a priority. But we also wrote this book for people who work in those institutions, and we hope it can serve as a blueprint for where you take this fight in the future. While the news media, lawmakers and most people you know continue to remain silent, you already have everything you need to begin the planning for the launch of a socially-engaged start up with a sign that says, quite simply, child adversity and maltreatment ends here. Ask us how.

Chapter Ten

———————————

Experience being courageous preferred, but not essential

A LOT HAS HAPPENED since we started this book project many moons ago. We have new jobs, new home bases, and a much clearer blueprint for how to get things done. We also have greater optimism, though as always it's tempered with caution.

We believe that if a measly quarter of the readers of this book responded to our calls to action we would soon see two major disruptions to business as usual.

First, we would start seeing email invites to rallies in front of city halls, county offices, and state houses, websites that demand real action, YouTube videos sharing stories around the emotional costs of trauma, new coalitions meeting weekly, and a linking of like-minded activists asking for local government, foundations, and nonprofits to fund and commit to data-driven, comprehensive, systemic, long-term ACEs prevention work.

Second, the work inside agencies would make some dramatic course corrections. Cutting through the bureaucratic dysfunction, activities would align with the mission (for a change). Helping kids is something we can all agree on, but ending ACEs is the way to do that. This would translate into the implementation of evidence-based strategies, within all family-serving government agencies, to produce measurable and meaningful results. Reforms would be guaranteed by in-your-face unrelenting activism at city meetings, town halls and online.

Most importantly to you, our reader, local systems would kick into gear to protect your children, your sister's children, and your neighbor's children. Equally important, the kids and families who live on the other less-resourced side of town would benefit from the same safeguards as your kids.

Within a few years, dots representing new ACEs prevention projects would light up a map on your tablet, a proud documentation of the national ACEs Prevention Network working in coordination with a robust mental health care network and revitalized child welfare system.

Only one thing prevents this from happening: Us. We, the writers and readers of this book, are only one ingredient vital to a recipe for comprehensive, local, data-driven ACEs prevention. We require people from all walks of life who are activists outside the system, or those working within it, to step up and do what's right.

Your role

We don't underestimate the cost of courage in the face of complacency, incompetence and corruption. Questioning a boss or a mayor is not something anyone looks forward to. We sure didn't. Change requires that we take chances and disrupt our lives. This means putting in evenings and weekends to form and run a local advocacy group. It means breaking chains of command at work and bypassing an obstructionist manager to get to a more reasonable person in upper management. It might mean leaving one job to take another where your efforts can be more impactful. Or you might find yourself moving to another city to head up some new effort, if given the opportunity to do work toward measurable results. It might mean using technology to expose unethical or illegal practice in government and nonprofit management. It more than likely means good old-fashioned whistleblowing.

For us, it meant working for many years on piloting new ways to use data and technology to solve problems once viewed as unsolvable in child welfare systems, and documenting the process in the how-to-get-it-done book you hold in your hand.

The good news is that work addressing the root causes of ACEs is underway, and you're invited to join. The rewards are nothing less than a nation where every child is safe, healthy and resilient, and every parent, if needed, has access to trauma-informed care. When we commit our brainpower, passion, political will, and tech expertise to one reachable goal, every city will see the end of what was once considered a problem that could never be solved. We will one day celebrate the end of unending trauma, and you can share with the children in your life your role in such a noble accomplishment.

APPENDIX I
QUESTIONS TO ASK, PONDER, AND DEBATE

The following questions can serve as a catalyst for work study groups or book clubs. We recommend taking on one chapter per week or month and exploring attitudes, ideas, and steps for getting to meaningful solutions, whether one is within an institution like child welfare or public health, a nonprofit with limited funds to focus on youth development, the mayor's office staff, or a software company with a book club of socially-engaged designers.

CHAPTER ONE: Comfortably Numb
- How numb are we to news about childhood trauma and fatalities?
- What can we do to reduce the numbing influence of the mass media on all our screens?
- Who is doing any work related to advocating for the safety and health of children and families in your community?

CHAPTER TWO: An epidemic we prefer not to see
- How are ACEs like a virus? How are they different?
- Why are some people able to shrug off childhood adversity as "no big deal" while others are traumatized by it?
- What are the financial costs of childhood trauma that you can see in your everyday life?

CHAPTER THREE: Software, eggshells, and minefields: Illustrating the problem in all its glorious shame
- What do you think of the ACEs survey? Had you taken it before or even heard of it?
- Do you think it would be useful to have all late elementary, middle, and high school students take the ACEs survey? Why or why not?
- How useful are ACEs scores from middle school students versus a random sample of adults across your state?

CHAPTER FOUR: Our inheritance of horrors: The complex, chaotic, and invisible root causes of trauma

- How is brainstorming root causes for bad coffee in an office different from brainstorming the root causes of ACEs?
- If a root cause of ACEs is untreated mental health challenges, what data and research tell a story of the availability of your county's mental health services? (For both children and parents.)
- How do you think community norms are related to how parents can treat their children?
- What do you think are the root causes of childhood trauma in your community?

CHAPTER FIVE: An infant, a motel room, and a pile of needles: The impossible work of child welfare pros

- What do you know about your local child welfare office?
- Where can you easily access data on local maltreatment?
- Does your state or local child welfare office have a robust quality and planning department with the capacity to promote a framework and process like continuous quality improvement?
- Do people who work on the prevention of ACEs see themselves differently from those who work in child welfare preventing maltreatment? If so, how?

CHAPTER SIX: Trauma's fuel tank: The ongoing crisis in mental healthcare

- What are the challenges to providing behavioral health care to children and families?
- What are the benefits of having behavioral health care based in a school setting?
- What are attitudes about accessing "talk therapy" in all your communities? Is there any stigma discussing trauma-related problem with a counselor?
- How can we better promote the benefits of mental health care and treating ACEs?

CHAPTER SEVEN: Because this is America: Why your zip code should not determine your destiny

- What are the benefits of home visitation for parents in your community and county?
- What are the benefits of early childhood programs? What

are the challenges to accessing such programs?
- What are the benefits of having youth mentors? What strategies are used to recruit mentors?
- How can organizations that serve families become data-driven, cross-sector, and adopt a systematic approach to preventing childhood trauma?
- Which groups are tackling the long term work of creating access to safe housing, medical/dental care, transport, job training and family-centric schools?

CHAPTER EIGHT: There's an app for that (maybe): Healthy kids and the promises and perils of technology
- What would be the benefits of an app or site that published information about family-centric services available in your area?
- What are the benefits of having services rated by clients? (The way people rate hotels on Trip Advisor.)
- What are the benefits of creating an online environment that would tell us if the needs of our most vulnerable families were being met?
- How can you easily access data and research online related to ACEs and maltreatment?
- How do you start or strengthen an organization to ensure that we address risk factors in our most vulnerable communities?

CHAPTER NINE: Get the Data and Make a Plan: Why we all live in Santa Fe, New Mexico
- What do you need to strengthen ACEs prevention work and resiliency promotion work?
- How data-driven, cross-sector and systemic is the current ACEs prevention work? How do we strengthen it?
- What can be done to ensure that each state has dedicated staff positions and the resources to implement the data-driven prevention of childhood trauma and maltreatment?
- How can you train people in continuous quality improvement at your place of work?
- How do we use data to disrupt dysfunctional systems?
- What can you do about the lack of urgency for addressing childhood trauma and maltreatment?
- Why will some people and agencies fear using data?

CHAPTER TEN: Experience being courageous preferred, but not essential

- Why would it take courage to work on ACEs prevention?
- What other large social problems required courage and risk to solve?
- What is one social problem you see as solved that can serve as a model for addressing ACEs?
- What is your role in ending the epidemic of childhood trauma and maltreatment?

APPENDIX II
RESILIENT COMMUNITY EXPERIENCE SURVEY

How do you rate the following services in your community? The term "accessible" means affordable and/or not a burden to get to, and not subject to long waiting lists.

1. Mental health care services to provide counselors to speak with about emotional problems, treat depression and untreated mental health challenges, and address adverse childhood experiences and trauma

Very accessible / Accessible / Not very accessible / Not Accessible / Don't know

2. Medical and dental care to increase health, resiliency and longevity

Very accessible / Accessible / Not very accessible / Not Accessible / Don't know

3. Housing programs to prevent homelessness and provide a safe place if a home is unsafe

Very accessible / Accessible / Not very accessible / Not Accessible / Don't know

4. Food pantries and programs to reduce hunger

Very accessible / Accessible / Not very accessible / Not Accessible / Don't know

5. Public transport that ensures residents get to vital social services, work or school

Very accessible / Accessible / Not very accessible / Not Accessible / Don't know

6. Job training to provide access to jobs with livable wages

Very accessible / Accessible / Not very accessible / Not Accessible / Don't know

CONTINUES ON NEXT PAGE

7. Early childhood programs that strengthen early learning

Very accessible / Accessible / Not very accessible / Not Accessible / Don't know

8. Family-centered community schools. (Schools that offer support with academics, tutoring, family support, and health and social services, and do so before, during and after school, on weekends, and over summer break. They also offer counseling services and can screen students and family members for emotional trauma and mental health challenges, or refer them to local behavioral health care agencies.)

Very accessible / Accessible / Not very accessible / Not Accessible / Don't know

9. Parent supports, including home visitation and respite programs, to strengthen families and reduce the chance of childhood injury, trauma or maltreatment

Very accessible / Accessible / Not very accessible / Not Accessible / Don't know

10. Youth mentors to provide strong role models and support for every boy and girl

Very accessible / Accessible / Not very accessible / Not Accessible / Don't know

END NOTES

Chapter Two

Trauma definitions: The American Psychological Association defines trauma this way: Trauma is an emotional response to a terrible event like an accident, rape or natural disaster. Immediately after the event, shock and denial are typical. Longer term reactions include unpredictable emotions, flashbacks, strained relationships and even physical symptoms like headaches or nausea. While these feelings are normal, some people have difficulty moving on with their lives. Psychologists can help these individuals find constructive ways of managing their emotions. http://www.apa.org/topics/trauma/

Effects of trauma: Respondents who indicated they had been abused as children reported less secure childhood and adult relationships than their hyper-abused counterparts. They were also more depressed and more likely to use destructive behaviors in conflict situations http://www.sciencedirect.com/science/article/pii/S0145213497000628

Effects of trauma on physical health: http://journals.lww.com/psychosomaticmedicine/Abstract/2009/10000/A_Meta_Analytic_Review_of_the_Effects_of_Childhood.1.aspx

ACEs Survey general: https://www.samhsa.gov/capt/ practicing-effective-prevention/prevention-behavioral-health/adverse-childhood-experiences

Major findings on the ACEs survey: As the number of ACES increases, so does the following: alcoholism and alcohol abuse, chronic obstructive pulmonary disease, depression, fetal death, health-related quality of life, illicit drug use, ischemic heart disease, liver disease, poor work performance, financial stress, risk for intimate partner violence, multiple sex partners, sexually transmitted diseases, smoking, suicide attempts, unintended pregnancies, early initiation of smoking, early initiation of sexual activity, adolescent pregnancy, risk for sexual violence, and poor academic achievement, to name just a few. https://www.cdc.gov/violenceprevention/acestudy/

Trauma and incarceration: http://www.journalofjuvjustice.org/JOJJ0302/article01.htm

Trauma and health: https://www.ncbi.nlm.nih.gov/pmc/articles/PMC4617302/

Financial costs of childhood trauma: https://www.cdc.gov/violenceprevention/childmaltreatment/economiccost.html

Fundamental attribution error: Handbook of Social Psychology. Edited by John Delamater https://books.google.com/books?id=xnVAuljbRcQC&pg=PA488&lpg=PA488&dq=fundamental+attribution+error+handbook+of+social+psychology&source=bl&ots=m9yzuXiP_m&sig=Zvrimt33rZpU43zuw30jxNL4lLo&hl=en&sa=X&ved=0ahUKEwiPoITNm4LVAhXr44MKHe2qBoYQ6AEIUjAG#v=onepage&q=fundamental%20attribution%20error%20handbook%20of%20social%20psychology&f=false

Chapter Three

Census data: https://www.census.gov/data.html

ACEs Survey in general: https://www.cdc.gov/violenceprevention/acestudy/about.html

Sexual abuse statistics: https://www.acf.hhs.gov/sites/default/files/cb/cm2015.pdf#page=29 and https://www.cdc.gov/violenceprevention/acestudy/ace_brfss.html

Effects of trauma: http://www.sciencedirect.com/science/article/pii/S0145213403002138

Child neglect: https://www.acf.hhs.gov/sites/default/files/cb/cm2015.pdf#page=29

Food insecurity: https://www.ers.usda.gov/topics/food-nutrition-assistance/food-security-in-the-us/key-statistics-graphics.aspx#children

Neglect and physical abuse definitions: https://www.child welfare.gov/pubPDFs/define.pdf#page=2&view=

Mental health challenges: http://psycnet.apa.org/journals/bul/ 108/1/50/

ACEs state data: https://www.cdc.gov/mmwr/preview/mmwrht ml/mm5949a1.htm

Chapter Four

Teen pregnancy: https://www.cdc.gov/teenpregnancy/about/ind ex.htm

Cost of teen pregnancy: http://thenationalcampaign.org/why-it-matters/public-cost

Sweden: https://www.usnews.com/news/best-countries /sweden

Utah: https://www.bloomberg.com/view/articles/2017-0328/how -utah-keeps-the-american-dream-alive

Child welfare history: http://www.newyorker.com/magazine/2016 /02/01/baby-doe

Chapter Five

Caseloads: http://www.cwla.org/wp-content/uploads/2014 /05/ DirectServiceWEB.pdf

Permanency guidelines: https://www.acf.hhs.gov/sites/default/fil es/cb/combined_fr_document_may_2015.pdf

Foster Care ages: http://www.ncsl.org/research/humanservices/e xtending-foster-care-to-18.aspx#50-State Chart

Child welfare departments and prevention: https://fas.org/sg p/crs/misc/R43458.p

Maltreatment statistics: https://jamanetwork.com/journals/jama pediatrics/fullarticle/1876686

Chapter Six

Cost of jail: https://www.bjs.gov/content/pub/pdf/spe01.pdf The average annual operating cost per state inmate in 2001 was $22,650, or $62.05 per day.

Salaries of high school graduates: https://www.census.gov/prod /2002pubs/p23-210.pdf

Behavioral health practitioners: https://www.samhsa.gov /samhsaNewsLetter/Volume_22_Number_4/building_the_beha vioral_health_workforce/

Mental health and economic productivity: https://www.nami. org/Learn-More/Mental-Health-By-the-Numbers

Chapter Seven

Home visitation: https://homvee.acf.hhs.gov/Outcome/2/Reduc tions-in-Child-Maltreatment/4/1 and http://childandfamilyresea rch.org/publications/top5benefits-of-home-visiting/ and https:// ncfy.acf.hhs.gov/sites/default/files/docs/17975-The_Role_ of_Home-Visiting_Programs.pdf and https://www.ncbi.nlm.nih .gov/pmc/articles/PMC5280088/

Word usage in young children: http://news.stanford.edu /news/2014/february/fernald-AAAS-children-021414.html

Katherine Ortega Courtney has a PhD in experimental psychology from Texas Christian University, where she studied at the Institute of Behavioral Research. Dr. Ortega Courtney worked with the State of New Mexico for eight years, first as the Juvenile Justice Epidemiologist, then as Bureau Chief of the Child Protective Services Research, Assessment and Data Bureau. An advocate for data-informed decision-making, Dr. Courtney championed and co-developed the New Mexico Data Leaders for Child Welfare program. She has worked in policy and research, and has led community initiatives through her work at the Santa Fe Community Foundation and the New Mexico Early Childhood Development Partnership. She is also the co-author, with Dominic Cappello, of ***Anna, Age Eight: The data-driven prevention of childhood trauma and maltreatment***, which served as a catalyst for the development of the Anna, Age Eight Institute in Santa Fe, New Mexico, where she serves as co-director. Dr. Ortega Courtney and Cappello wrote the follow-up book ***100% Community*** to guide local leadership in every county in their work designing trauma-free and truly family-friendly cities and towns. Dr. Ortega Courtney serves as an advocate for strengthening continuous quality improvement in all family-serving organizations through the 100% Community initiative and 100% Community course, a data-driven, cross-sector and county-focused childhood trauma prevention strategy.

Dominic Cappello is a *New York Times* bestselling author and TEDx Conference curator with decades of experience advocating for health, safety and education. He has a Master of Arts in Liberal Studies with an emphasis in language and communication from Regis University. He worked for the New Mexico Department of Health Epidemiology and Response Division and the state Child Protective Services Research, Assessment and Data Bureau, where he co-developed the Data Leaders for Child Welfare program, which he implemented in New York City, Connecticut and New Mexico. Cappello is the creator of the *Ten Talks* book series on family safety that gained a national audience when he discussed his work on *The Oprah Winfrey Show*. He is also the co-author, with Dr. Katherine Ortega Courtney, of ***Anna, Age Eight: The data-driven prevention of childhood trauma and maltreatment***, which served as a catalyst for the development of the Anna, Age Eight Institute in Santa Fe, New Mexico, where he serves as co-director. Cappello and Dr. Ortega Courtney wrote the follow up book *100% Community* to guide local leadership in every county in their work designing trauma-free and truly family-friendly cities and towns. Through the ***100% Community*** initiative and course, Cappello advocates for data-driven, technology-empowered, and systematic approaches to ensuring safe childhoods and thriving students, families and local economies.

Connect with us: Anna, Age Eight Institute – AnnaAgeEight.org.

Made in the USA
San Bernardino, CA
19 January 2020